Contemporary British Dramatists, Volume VII:

THE FANATICS

CONTEMPORARY BRITISH DRAMATISTS

Newest titles

THE MARQUISE. By NOEL COWARD

ONE MORE RIVER. By ASHLEY DUKES
" Mr. Dukes's comedy is noteworthy."—" T.P.'s & Cassell's Weekly."

ISABEL'S ELEVEN. By H. F. RUBINSTEIN

THE IRON DUKE. By A. J. TALBOT
" 'The Iron Duke' is the best chronicle play of our generation."—" Daily Telegraph."

DISTINGUISHED VILLA. By KATE O'BRIEN
" Miss O'Brien has achieved a good play."—" London Mercury."

YESTERDAY. By MARGARET MACNAMARA

THREE ONE-ACT PLAYS. By H. M. HARWOOD

A SOCIAL CONVENIENCE. By H. M. HARWOOD

THE HOUSE. By H. F. RUBINSTEIN

MERRILEON WISE. By MILES MALLESON

CONFLICT. By MILES MALLESON. (2nd Impression.)
" Cries out of its own quality to be put on the stage."—" T.P.'s & Cassell's Weekly."

THIS WOMAN BUSINESS. By BEN W. LEVY. (2nd Impression.)
" A pure delight."—" Morning Post."
" May turn out to be a genius."—St. John Ervine.

THE MULLIGATAWNY MEDALLION. By BARRINGTON GATES
" Mr. Gates knows his stage and has a keen sense of situation."—" Glasgow Herald."

THE SPORT OF GODS. By JOHN COURNOS

THE WIDOW'S CRUISE. By JOAN TEMPLE
" A really notable first piece."—" Morning Post."

MR. GODLY BESIDE HIMSELF. By GERALD BULLETT

THE MAN WHO WAS THURSDAY. By MRS. CECIL CHESTERTON & RALPH NEALE

THE OFFENCE. By MORDAUNT SHAIRP
" A great play ? . . . something very near."—B. M. H. in the " Daily Express."

(Continued on page 126.)

THE FANATICS

A COMEDY IN THREE ACTS

By MILES MALLESON

"*I believe you've got to have something of a fanatic in you to do anything worth while these days. The thing is to keep one's fanaticism and to keep one's humanity.*"

LONDON

ERNEST BENN LIMITED

Bouverie House, Fleet Street

1927

MADE AND PRINTED IN GREAT BRITAIN

First published February 1924
Second Edition April 1927
Second Impression (Second Edition) April 1927

NOTE

At the first performance of the production at the Ambassadors Theatre several extensive cuts were made, and for particulars of these cuts for acting purposes application should be made to the author, c/o Messrs. Curtis Brown, Ltd., 6, Henrietta Street, Covent Garden, W.C.2.

TO THOSE WHO LIKE THE PLAY

PERSONS OF THE PLAY

MR. FREEMAN
MRS. FREEMAN
JOHN, *their son.*
GWEN, *their daughter.*
COLIN MACKENZIE
FRANCES SEWELL
MARGARET HEAL
TOBY
ROSIE

SCENE: *Mr. Freeman's Home.*

ACT I   *Downstairs.*
ACT II   *Upstairs.*
ACT III *Downstairs again.*

TIME: *The Present.*

ACT I

ACT I

Downstairs

All that follows takes place at MR. FREEMAN'S *house in the neighbourhood of Lancaster Gate; a large house in a terrace of others like it. It begins in the dining-room; middle-class, but sumptuously so. Dinner is in its final stages; a decanter of port is on the table, and a goodly array of the best fruits to be bought.* MR. FREEMAN *is seated at the table very occupied with a fruit;* MRS. FREEMAN *sits opposite to him; there is no one else in the room.* MR. FREEMAN *is rather short and rather round, a little red and a little bald;* MRS. FREEMAN *is his wife.*

MR. FREEMAN *continues to eat his fruit—there is no other sound.*

MR. FREEMAN (*when his mouth is unoccupied*): Disgusting! (*He reaches out and selects another fruit.*) Makes me *sick!*

[*The door opens and such an attractive head comes round it.*

THE HEAD: *No!* . . . He hasn't.

[*The head withdraws and the door shuts.*

MR. FREEMAN: *Abominable!* I wonder if Florence knows.

MRS. FREEMAN: She's out.

MR. FREEMAN: Rosie then. (*Calling.*) Gwen! . . . Gwen!!

[*The door reopens and the head reappears.*

MR. FREEMAN: Does Rosie know?

9

THE HEAD: No.

[*The head disappears and the door shuts.*

MR. FREEMAN: *Monstrous!* (*Then suddenly he shouts again*) HI! Gwen! . . . Gwen!!

[*The door reopens and the head reappears.*

THE HEAD: Yes?

[*For answer* MR. FREEMAN *angles for his keys in his hip pocket, catches them with a laborious spasm and throws them on to the table.*

MR. FREEMAN: Liqueur.

[*The owner of the head comes into the room.* GWEN, *the daughter; twenty-four years old, and very attractive. She comes straight to the table, picks up the keys, and unlocks a cupboard in a handsome sideboard.*

MRS. FREEMAN: Shut the door, dear.

[GWEN *goes and shuts the door.*

It's cold.

[GWEN *returns to the cupboard.*

GWEN: Which?

MR. FREEMAN: Benedictine. . . . No. Chartreuse.

GWEN: Green?

MR. FREEMAN: Yellow. . . . What's the time? (*But he gets no answer.*) Nobody in this house ever knows what the time is. (*So he looks at his own watch.*) D'Ha! He won't be back to dinner now. . . . (*He selects a cigar from a box on the table*) . . . preposterous.

MRS. FREEMAN: You're worried.

Mr. Freeman: Of course I'm worried . . . he left the office three-quarters of an hour too early for lunch, and he never came back at all. I haven't set eyes on him.

Mrs. Freeman: He came home.

Mr. Freeman: Eh? What excuse did he give?

Mrs. Freeman: I only heard him upstairs in his attic . . . playing the piano.

Mr. Freeman: *Playing the piano!!!* I ask you . . . a grown man . . . what is 'e? Twenty-six.

Mrs. Freeman: Twenty-eight.

Mr. Freeman: Nonsense. (*Then he considers.*) Oh, yes, twenty-eight. He walks calmly out of his office in the City in the middle of the morning, he leaves an afternoon's work untouched and he comes home and PLAYS THE PIANO.

Mrs. Freeman: He was always fond of music.

Mr. Freeman: *I'm* fond of music, but if I was to behave like that I'd be playing a barrel organ in a fortnight . . . where you going?

[Gwen *has given him his liqueur, relocked the cupboard, put the keys back on the table, and is going quietly out of the room; her father's question is mere family curiosity.*

Gwen: Drawing-room—going to read.

[*She goes out.*

Mrs. Freeman (*when the door has closed safely*): I've got something on my mind, too.

Mr. Freeman: What about?

MRS. FREEMAN: About him.

MR. FREEMAN: What?

[*In answer* MRS. FREEMAN *goes to a writing-desk. He continues his own train of thought.*

He's not worth a damn in the office. He could be. (*His indignation increases.*) He walks in an hour late, he walks out an hour early, and he never walks back at all. . . . No "whys," no "wherefores" . . . when I think of all that I've done for that boy . . . (*He becomes conscious that the hand that isn't holding a cigar is holding a letter*) . . . What's this?

MRS. FREEMAN: Smell it.

MR. FREEMAN: Filthy . . . what's wrong with it? . . . only scent, isn't it?

MRS. FREEMAN: It isn't Frankie's writing.

[MR. FREEMAN *consults it.*

He left it about . . . he's had others like it . . . he's told Rosie to take them straight upstairs to him.

MR. FREEMAN: Rosie tell you?

MRS. FREEMAN: I've noticed.

MR. FREEMAN: What John does in his spare time is nothing to do with me. It's not his spare time I'm bothered about . . . it's his working life.

MRS. FREEMAN: He *is* engaged to Frankie . . . suppose there should be anything serious with this other girl.

MR. FREEMAN: What other girl?

MRS. FREEMAN: *Somebody* writes those letters.

MR. FREEMAN: . . . Um. . . . I shouldn't worry . . . he's not quite a fool. . . . Leave it to me. I'll give him this.

MRS. FREEMAN: He's not happy.

MR. FREEMAN: If a man neglects his work as John's doing, he can't expect to be happy.

MRS. FREEMAN: Has he told you he isn't going to spend Christmas with us?

MR. FREEMAN: Where's he going . . .?

MRS. FREEMAN: To stay with Mr. . . . I don't know his name . . . his friend.

MR. FREEMAN: Funny-lookin' feller . . . always in the house. *I* know. That's another thing; who *is* this feller? . . . I don't know.

MRS. FREEMAN (*taking her son's part*): He's always had the attic for his own . . . hasn't he? . . . with his own friends.

MR. FREEMAN: I know. I've never interfered. I've no wish to interfere . . . when he was a baby in the nursery up there—or a schoolboy with his friends, but now . . . here's this feller . . . he called yesterday when John was out—I met him on the stairs . . . didn't know him from Adam; we grinned . . . dam' silly. . . . Hullo!

[*There has been a prolonged moaning wailing sound —like the cry of some agonised ghost.* MR. FREEMAN *hurries to the window.*

It's Frankie . . . in the new car; with her father. Hullo! How are you! (*He waves cordially. The window*

13

being shut there is not the remotest chance of his being heard.)
Hullo, Frankie . . . pretty girl she's getting. (*He comes away from the window.*) 'Spose she's come for John. I shall speak to him to-night, when he comes in.

Mrs. Freeman: I shouldn't say too much about his friend upstairs.

Mr. Freeman: Um?

Mrs. Freeman: Well, we did make the arrangement he should be private upstairs—as if it were his own flat.

Mr. Freeman: I don't suppose I've been up there for a year.

Mrs. Freeman: Nor have I . . . he might take a flat of his own. I shouldn't like that.

[Rosie, *a picturesque little parlour-maid, shows in* Frankie Sewell. *She is a pretty girl of twenty-four or so, and is very good at tennis and hockey.*

Mrs. Freeman: Well, Frankie dear.

Frankie: Good evening, Mrs. Freeman.

[*They kiss.*

Mr. Freeman: What have you done with your father?

Frankie: He couldn't come in; he's going to call back for me.

Mr. Freeman: Your young man isn't in.

Frankie: Isn't he?

[*Again the cry of the agonised ghost.*

Frankie: Your gate's in awfully good voice to-night.

Mr. Freeman (*who has gone to the window*): Wants oil.

DOWNSTAIRS

FRANKIE (*at a bowl of chocolates on the table*): May I?

MRS. FREEMAN: Of course, dear.

FRANKIE: Thank you.

MR. FREEMAN (*back from the window; aside to his wife*): It's John. Take her into the drawing-room.

MRS. FREEMAN: Let's join Gwen, dear. It's so much nicer in the drawing-room. Bring the chocolates if you like.

FRANKIE: Oh no, thanks; I'll take one more, though.

MR. FREEMAN: I'll be with you in a minute.

MRS. FREEMAN (*ushering* FRANKIE *out*): Gwen'll be so pleased. She's only reading.

[MR. FREEMAN *rings . . .* ROSIE *appears.*

MR. FREEMAN: Mr. John's just come in. Tell him I want him in here.

ROSIE: Yessir.

[*She withdraws.*

[MR. FREEMAN *waits.*

[*To him enters his son* JOHN; *well-dressed in a lounge suit evidently cut by a good West-end tailor; well-built, and nice-looking; with a pleasant-sounding voice.*

MR. FREEMAN: Come in—I want to speak to you.

[JOHN *comes in and shuts the door, but* MR. FREEMAN *doesn't speak at once, so, after a moment,* JOHN *does. He speaks quietly.*

JOHN: Whose car's that outside?

MR. FREEMAN: The Sewells'.

JOHN (*with quick concern*): Is Frankie here?

MR. FREEMAN: Yes.

JOHN: Where?

MR. FREEMAN: Drawing-room.

JOHN (*evidently upset*): She said she wasn't coming round to-night.

MR. FREEMAN: You ought to have let your mother know you weren't coming back to dinner.

JOHN (*puzzled*): But . . . surely . . . I thought you were all going out to dinner with the Cleavers.

MR. FREEMAN: To-morrow night.

JOHN: I've made a mistake.

MR. FREEMAN: You have . . . had your dinner?

JOHN: Yes.

MR. FREEMAN: Restaurant?

JOHN: Yes.

MR. FREEMAN: Some girl, I suppose?

JOHN: I was by myself.

MR. FREEMAN: Then why on earth didn't you come home?

[JOHN *doesn't answer; after a searching look at him his father continues.*

Of course, if you prefer your own company, that's nothing to do with me, but your life from ten o'clock in the morning till five in the evening *does* belong to me. (*In answer to a look from his son he expands that.*) It belongs to the firm. Now look here, young man, I can put this in a nutshell. You've been engaged to Frankie some time, on the understanding I make you a junior partner when you marry.

JOHN: Yes.

MR. FREEMAN: How much do you get now?

JOHN: You know.

MR. FREEMAN: Five hundred a year. A thousand when you marry; and a yearly rise after that. Of course your life belongs to the firm—and will do, more and more. It's about time you realised that.

JOHN: I realise it all right.

MR. FREEMAN: Then I want to know why you left the office an hour before lunch—and never came back after lunch.

JOHN: . . . It's difficult to explain.

MR. FREEMAN: I daresay it is; but it's the sort of thing that's got to be explained.

JOHN: I don't think you understand.

MR. FREEMAN: I daresay I shan't—but I'll have a dam' good try. I'm not quite a fool, though you think I am . . . any other man employed in the firm who did what you've done to-day without good reason would get the sack. I want to know your reason. Exactly.

JOHN: It will sound very trivial.

MR. FREEMAN: That doesn't matter . . . I'm waiting.

JOHN: I'm trying to write.

B   17

MR. FREEMAN: What d'you mean—" write "?

JOHN: Articles; and a book——

MR. FREEMAN: What about?

JOHN: . . . the world in general.

MR. FREEMAN: What for?

JOHN: I want to. I got stuck—this morning in the office, I got an idea that I thought might unstick me . . . I only meant to go out for a walk for a few minutes, but it came so clear in my head that I came home and worked.

MR. FREEMAN: You were playing the piano.

JOHN: Strumming between whiles.

MR. FREEMAN: I see . . . now look here . . . I've got no objection to your writing articles, or whatever it is and strumming on the piano—it's a very nice thing to be able to do . . . these things may be all very well in their place—but their place is not the best working hours of your life . . . that's what you've got to understand. Now, listen to me, my boy, you've got a *niche*.

JOHN: I've got a what?

MR. FREEMAN: A NICHE—will you please not laugh.

JOHN: I beg your pardon; it sounded comic.

MR. FREEMAN: Well, it isn't comic. You've got a very pretty little income waiting for you; and a prettier little wife, but if you think you're going to inherit the whole show mooning away a few hours at the office, when it happens to suit you, because I and others work hard for you there all day—*and have done for the best part of our lives*—you're vastly mistaken. The business is your bread and butter; your life; and you've got to give the best part of your life to it; you get an idea in your head, and that Robinson contract cropped up in the afternoon, and you precious nearly lost the firm a thousand pounds . . . what have you got to say to that?

    [*The atmosphere is changing; the argument is degenerating into the family row.*

Well, what have you got to say to that?

JOHN: This afternoon my own work seemed most important.

MR. FREEMAN: You're a perfect dam' fool: *work!* You've got no sense of values.

JOHN: We've a *different* sense of values.

MR. FREEMAN: I'm not going to argue. It's not going to happen again; do you grasp that?

JOHN: Need we discuss it to-night?

MR. FREEMAN: There's no discussing to be done.

JOHN: I'm sorry. I see your point of view.

MR. FREEMAN: That's splendid.

JOHN: But——

MR. FREEMAN: But what?

    [*The wailing gate intervenes*—JOHN *hurries to the window.*

MR. FREEMAN: Who's that?

JOHN: For me.

    [MR. FREEMAN *goes to the window to look.*

MR. FREEMAN: Who *is* this feller?

JOHN: He's part of my private life. . . .

MR. FREEMAN: I daresay—but I can't have your private life swarming all over my house. I can't walk out of a room without falling over a perfect stranger.

JOHN (*going to the door, opening, and speaking out of it*): Rosie . . . show my friend in here, please.

MR. FREEMAN: I've never interfered; I've no wish to interfere, but——

[ROSIE *shows in the gentleman;* MR. FREEMAN *having his back to the door goes on talking.*

——hang it all, if this feller's going to spend half his time under my roof, I might at least know what to call him when we bump in the passage——

JOHN: Let me introduce you—Colin Mackenzie . . . my father.

MR. FREEMAN: Oh! . . . How d'you do? How d'you do? (*He shakes hands.*) Glad to make your acquaintance. I was just telling my boy here, I should like to—one likes to show a little decent hospitality.

COLIN: Thank you.

MR. FREEMAN: Sit down, won't you, sit down.

COLIN: Thank you.

[*A little silence.*

JOHN: I believe you saw Colin's play the other night . . . didn't you go to the Criterion?—" A Pair of Pyjamas "——

MR. FREEMAN: Yes?

JOHN: The author!

MR. FREEMAN: Really!? By jove . . . did you really write it?

COLIN: Yes.

MR. FREEMAN: By jove yes . . . my wife and I enjoyed it immensely . . . most amusin' . . . *most amusin'*. . . . By jove! . . . it's a great success, isn't it?

COLIN: It's been on some time.

JOHN: A year; *and* in America; *and* three touring companies; *and* in the colonies; *and* the world's film rights.

MR. FREEMAN (*offering the box of cigars*): Try one o' these?

COLIN: Thanks.

MR. FREEMAN: Have a drink?

COLIN: No, thanks.

MR. FREEMAN: Wouldn't you like to come into the drawing-room? . . . my wife would be delighted to meet you . . . she really did enjoy it immensely—very funny —very funny indeed—immensely.

JOHN (*cutting in*): I'm going to take him upstairs. He's been away and I've been away; we haven't seen one another for months.

MR. FREEMAN (*rising*): Well, I'm glad to have met you. I hope you'll look in again one evening.

COLIN (*rising to shake hands*): Thank you.

MR. FREEMAN (*going*): See you again, John . . . don't forget Frankie's here. Good night.

21

COLIN: Good night.

[MR. FREEMAN *goes.*

JOHN (*at once*): Come upstairs.

COLIN: I can't stay. I want to borrow your score of the new ballet. At least Margaret does. I'm taking her to hear it.

JOHN: It's upstairs.

COLIN: They're doing it last. I needn't go for a few minutes.

JOHN: Then you'd better have a drink.

COLIN: Right.

JOHN: Whiskey?

COLIN: Thanks.

JOHN: Have a good holiday?

COLIN: Yes.

JOHN: It's nearly three months since I've seen you. How's life?

COLIN: Very good. (*He gets his drink.*) Thanks. And with you?

JOHN: Rotten.

COLIN: Why?

JOHN (*with some deliberation*): We only have a certain amount of energy and vitality in us, Colin; and I'm using mine up on things that are utterly unimportant.

COLIN: The same tack you were on last time I saw you?

JOHN: Yes.

COLIN: You're not going to get much sympathy out of me.

JOHN: Oh! . . . . why?

COLIN: John! You can overdo ideals . . . they can make one rather useless and a little bit silly. . . . I've been thinking about you a good deal while I've been away. . . . I'd made up my mind to tell you what I thought of you one of these days.

JOHN: Now, please. I'm in no mood to wait.

COLIN: Well——

JOHN: Come on; out with it; what have you been thinking? What's wrong with me?

[*There is a certain eager impatience in his manner.*

COLIN: Well—to be quite frank with you—I think all this talk about the business being a waste of your life is rather stupid. The world's in a devil of a mess; we're all living on a volcano; but, as far as one can be sure of anything, your business is sure; you get a very good screw; you get all your evenings to yourself; in a world where ninety per cent of people are continually anxious about their livelihood, your comfort and comparative wealth are assured. You're a damned lucky man, John, and you've got no right to go about grousing about yourself.

JOHN: Can I be quite frank answering that?

COLIN: Of course.

JOHN: There's one big difference between us.

COLIN: Yes?

JOHN: It's difficult to say.

COLIN: Don't be a fool.

JOHN: You never went into the trenches.

[*This causes a sudden stoppage in the dialogue, momentary but the severance is complete; it doesn't go on in quite the same tone afterwards.*

COLIN: No. I agree to that difference—very humbly; but I don't see what difference that makes about the business.

JOHN: It makes the hell of a difference to *me* . . . it's hateful to talk about it . . . but there it is.

COLIN (*gently*): I'm interested.

JOHN (*responding*): There were several of us, Colin, who used to talk about the whole thing out there; I mean, why the whole thing had happened, and what we were going to do about it when it was over . . . a good many of us to start with . . . we got fewer; the lucky ones were killed outright. Jack Bardsley got half his face blown away and *can't* talk now; Peter Glen's blind; Chris—Chris was engaged to a most attractive girl . . . he was mad about her . . . used to talk to her at night . . . I heard him once, when he thought I was asleep—he got a bit of shrapnel in his stomach and thighs, and had to be cut away. He never married. Little Westerby's mad. . . . I'm the only one left. . . . Sometimes I think I've got no right to be alive at all, Colin—just a fluke . . . there are millions of my age, skull and bone and rotting flesh just under the earth over there. . . .

[COLIN *has no answer . . . the short silence is tense . . . then he goes on more calmly.*

If the war hadn't happened I should have married Frankie; and gone into the business, and settled down to it . . . but I *can't* just go on using my life up aimlessly— or what seems to me aimlessly, as if nothing had happened . . . to hear them talk—father and his lot, you'd think nothing had happened—*my God!*

It's hard to talk about it; it's hard to feel a thing very deeply, and talk about it, and not sound priggish; but I must talk to somebody; you're the only one.

COLIN: Thank you.

JOHN: You're an idealist, really. You wrote " A Pair of Pyjamas," and you've made the devil of a lot of money, but you know the real worth of things; that's why you get angry with me when I still care about ideals; it makes you uncomfortable; and you hate being uncomfortable, because you've made too much money.

COLIN: I shall have another of your drinks and then I shall go.

JOHN: For the love of God, don't! Not till you need. Colin, things can't go on like they are with me, I want your advice.

COLIN: Are you doing any writing?

JOHN: Yes; of course.

COLIN: You ought to stick to the business, and do your own work in the evenings.

JOHN: . . . We fought like hell out there all day and all night; we didn't just let off a few guns in the evenings, as a sort of hobby, after we'd spent the day doing something else. If we're going to have any sort of world for our children after those years of bloody slaughter, it seems to me we've got to fight like hell all the time now. It's no good writing anything unconsidered these days. One must read, and think, and meet people, and be quiet. . . . You can't serve God and Mammon. There are some jolly good things in that book; Colin, it's dreadful to spend one's best energies doing something, when you feel you ought to be doing something else.

COLIN: You've got an Urge.

JOHN: I've got something horrible. My father told me it was a Niche: you say it's a Nurge!

COLIN: It's what Quakers get. The spirit urges and they feel wicked if they don't follow.

JOHN: I feel miserable.

COLIN: Same thing.

JOHN: And, incidentally, while I mess on day after day, I'm getting my life into more of a muddle. I feel a cad about Frankie, and I feel a cad about Toby; I really don't know what I ought to do about either of them.

COLIN: You're engaged to Frankie?

JOHN: Before I went to France. The daughter of my father's partner; both families delighted; and they've all taken it up at the point where it was left off as if it was just the same; it isn't, nothing's just the same . . . for one thing when I was engaged I was innocent .   quite . . . one learnt more than soldiering in France.

COLIN: I don't know why you should put *that* down to the war—it happens to some of us even in peace time.

JOHN: It complicates things.

COLIN: How?

DOWNSTAIRS

JOHN: In the old days Frankie and I used to go about together a lot—like any respectably engaged couple.

COLIN: Yes?

JOHN: I used to take her to the theatre, and straight back to her house afterwards; her mother couldn't sleep unless she knew Frankie was in; and I always said good night to her on her doorstep with a kiss—quite a nice one, but perfectly respectable.

COLIN: Yes.

JOHN: That was all. I don't say I never wanted any more. However, I didn't expect any more; I didn't know any more, and I was quite ready to go on like that till we were married.

COLIN: Yes?

JOHN: I was terrified of getting killed in France before I'd had any experience at all.

COLIN: Yes.

JOHN: Just before an attack, when I was quite sure I was going to get knocked out, I went off the deep end and had my experience.

COLIN: Yes.

JOHN: Then we attacked . . . it was funny; I remember feeling very proud of myself—and I didn't get knocked out. Afterwards I thought a great deal about that first little French girl, and about Frankie; and one night I realised I loved Frankie desperately, because I wanted her like that; and because of Frankie I kept clear of any more of it. . . . I just lived for my next leave, and the moment when I should see Frankie again . . .

27

and the first time we were alone again—it was in this room—I was standing over there and she came in, and came towards me and I went to meet her, and I put my arms round her and held her close—closer than I'd ever done before. My God, I loved her that moment. . . .

COLIN: Yes?

JOHN: She pushed me away. She hardly said anything; but she made me feel that she was a little angry and a little indignant—I've never felt such a fool in my life . . . before I went back to the front that leave, I'd met Toby.

COLIN: I remember. You still see her?

JOHN: Sometimes. She's coming here to-night.

COLIN: Here!

JOHN: Upstairs. It's like my own flat, you know.

COLIN: Yes—but . . .

JOHN: I know. But I was certain they were all going out to dinner. And she's always wanted to see the attic; and they haven't gone out; and now Frankie's turned up!

COLIN: Frankie!

JOHN: Yes; she's in the drawing-room; I'm worried.

COLIN: I'm not surprised.

JOHN: I'm desperately anxious to get Toby up there without her meeting anybody. It's an underhand business; it's got to stop. (*He is troubled.*) They've never been so close; in any sort of way. . . . Colin, I don't make love to Frankie; not at all; she doesn't seem to want it.

COLIN: Are you sure?

JOHN: Yes, I think so; that's the trouble. I never get any *response* from her. It makes me rather uncomfortable with her, and shy! She doesn't seem to miss anything . . . but, unless, in my marriage, that part of it is as perfect, and as beautiful as . . . as Toby has taught me it can be, my marriage will be a failure. I'm getting afraid it isn't in Frankie.

COLIN: It may be. You never can tell.

JOHN: And it may not be . . . a mistaken marriage messes up two lives at least.

COLIN: But they're not uncommon.

JOHN: It's silly, isn't it?

COLIN: But there it is.

JOHN: Do you know what I believe I *ought* to do?

COLIN: What?

JOHN: Go to Frankie and either break off our engagement, or else ask her to come away with me somewhere. . . I'm perfectly serious; you may say "There it is . . . it's the way Civilisation has always managed it." Civilisation made millions of young people kill and maim and torture one another for five bloody years—there's something wrong with Civilisation. I don't mean that because a thing was there before the war it *must* be wrong —but it *may* be . . . a good many things have got to be thought out again from the beginning—this business of marriage is one of them.

COLIN: Have you said anything about it to her?

JOHN: No.

COLIN: Why don't you?

[GWEN *comes quickly into the room.*

GWEN: Oh! sorry; I thought you were upstairs.

JOHN: Come in. You do know one another, don't you?

COLIN: Yes. We've met. How d'you do?

[*They shake hands.*

JOHN: I'll get that score. (*He moves to the door.*)

COLIN (*to* GWEN): I wonder if you remember where we met?

GWEN: Quite well; at a concert; you were very nice to me.

COLIN: I'm very glad.

GWEN: A man played some very modern music—and you asked me what I thought of it; I didn't like it a bit really, but I didn't like to say so; and you said it was the sort of music one never ought to hear for the first time.

COLIN: Not such a bad remark; I wonder where I heard it . . . do you play and sing, and have your brothers accomplishments?

GWEN: I don't do anything.

JOHN (*who has stopped to select a fruit from the table—as he disappears*): Painting's Gwen's forte.

COLIN: Painting?

GWEN: I've given it up. . . .

COLIN: Why?

GWEN: I don't know.

COLIN: I should like to see something of yours.

GWEN: That's mine. (*She indicates a little painting on the wall that is hung close to another. . . . He goes to it.*) I was very young.

COLIN: It's very good.

GWEN: I used to love painting.

COLIN (*moving to the other picture*): This yours too?

GWEN: No; that's by . . . somebody else.

[*He looks at her—and back at the picture.*

COLIN (*meaning it*): It's quite beautiful.

GWEN (*with eagerness*): Do you think so? . . . I do.

COLIN: It's not unlike yours . . . you knew the painter?

GWEN (*simply*): I wanted to marry him . . . only . . . well, he was quite poor, so it was stopped. And then he was killed.

COLIN: In the war?

GWEN: Yes.

COLIN: I'm sorry.

GWEN: I've got over it. I didn't think I should—but I have.

[*They look at each other and smile.*

COLIN: Why has your brother kept us apart all this time?

GWEN: Has he?

COLIN: I know him so well; it seems absurd I know you so little.

GWEN: Well—here I am!

COLIN: And I've got to rush away; I'm sorry——

GWEN: So am I.

COLIN: I'm going to hear this new ballet: I wish you were coming.

GWEN: So do I.

COLIN: I'm taking somebody. I've got the last two seats in the house. . . . Will you come to-morrow night?

GWEN: Yes.

COLIN: Do you go to bed very early?

GWEN (*laughing*): Why?

COLIN: If I come in after the ballet—to tell you whether I've got tickets—will you have disappeared?

GWEN: No.

[JOHN *returns with the music score.*

COLIN: Thanks . . . I must be off. . . . (*To* GWEN) Then I won't say good night. . . . John, I'm going to look in on my way back from the show.

JOHN: Do . . . bring Margaret . . . what time does this thing begin?

[*They disappear.* . . . GWEN *is quiet in the room till her brother's return.*

JOHN: If you're going into the drawing-room, I wish you'd tell Frankie I want to see her.

GWEN: Is he married?

JOHN: Colin?

GWEN: Yes.

JOHN: No.

GWEN: Does he live by himself?

JOHN: Er . . . as a matter of fact I believe he does, at the moment.

GWEN (*point-blank*): What's that mean, Jacko?

JOHN (*a little taken aback*): Well—he's made a lot of money; he's got a beautiful flat and a lovely little cottage in the country; he knows lots of people; there's a queer superficial cynicism about him—but if I was in trouble I'd sooner go to him than to anybody I know——

GWEN: Yes? . . . Go on.

JOHN: He married when he was quite young; about twenty I believe and it failed; I think he divorced her; he's never found anything permanent since.

[ROSIE *enters to clear the table.*

In some ways I think he's a very lonely person, but he's not always alone.

GWEN (*moving to the door*): I'll tell Frankie you want her.

JOHN (*as she is at the door*): Not in the attic. Down here.

GWEN: Right.

[*She goes.*

JOHN (*to* ROSIE, *who is clearing away*): You'll show my friend straight up into the attic, Rosie, when she comes—won't you?

ROSIE: Yes, Mr. John.

JOHN: Is that speaking-tube arrangement mended yet?

ROSIE: Yes, Mr. John.

c

JOHN: . . . If I'm up there when Miss Frankie is going you might give me a whistle on it, will you? . . . don't wait for an answer . . . just blow it three times and I'll know what it means.

ROSIE: Yes, Mr. John.

JOHN: Thank you.

[FRANKIE *comes in.*

FRANKIE: Do you want me?

JOHN: Yes . . . don't bother about the table now, Rosie, d'you mind——?

ROSIE: No, Mr. John.

JOHN: I'll ring later.

ROSIE: Thank you, sir.

[ROSIE *goes out.*

JOHN: Another row with my father to-night.

FRANKIE: Oh, John! . . .

JOHN: He was in the right.

FRANKIE: What about?

JOHN: I stayed away from the office.

FRANKIE: Why did you?

JOHN: What would you say if I chucked it altogether?

FRANKIE: The business?

JOHN: Yes.

FRANKIE: For good?

JOHN: Yes.

FRANKIE: What would you do?

34

JOHN: Oh, there's a lot of writing I want to get done.

FRANKIE: What sort of writing?

JOHN (*wretched*): Oh . . . articles; and a book.

FRANKIE: To get it published?

JOHN: I hope so.

FRANKIE: Would you get any money for it?

JOHN: Not much.

FRANKIE: Then what would happen to us?

JOHN: . . . I don't know the answer to that.

FRANKIE: John—what's the matter? . . . do you mean you want a longer holiday?

JOHN: I want to start work.

FRANKIE: But you *can't* talk about giving up the business . . . after all it's going to make our marriage possible, isn't it——?

JOHN: Are you looking forward to our marriage?

FRANKIE: I should think I *am!*

JOHN: Are you *really?*

FRANKIE: John! . . . (*She goes to him and stands quite close to him, playing with the lapel of his coat . . . her voice is thrillingly low and eager.*) I've been thinking such lots about the time when we're married.

JOHN: Have you?

FRANKIE: Yes. Listen! . . . If we don't furnish those two top rooms at once, I think we'll be able to have two servants; I've been going all through it with mother to-day—my dear, the prices of things are awful—but that'll mean one to wait at dinner, and that's ever so much nicer—and I'm going to give you such lovely little dinners—when you bring your friends home—and p'r'aps when you don't sometimes! . . . Oh, and I've furnished your study to-day in my head—it's going to be ever so comfy . . . and you can write your book there in the evenings . . . I won't come near you if you don't want me to . . . you know, dear, we couldn't have a smaller house than the little one at the corner, could we? . . . and it's really ever so cheap.

JOHN: It's a queer business, marriage, isn't it?

FRANKIE: Yes.

JOHN: We've got to be everything to each other for the rest of our lives.

FRANKIE: Dear! . . . I'm going to try to be——

JOHN: . . . Frankie!

FRANKIE: Yes, dear.

JOHN: Do you remember once when I took you in my arms and kissed you?

FRANKIE: Yes.

JOHN: You *do* remember that time?

FRANKIE (*low*): Yes. Very well.

JOHN: If I did it now—would you tell me not to?

FRANKIE: . . . I don't know.

JOHN: May I?

FRANKIE: I'd rather you didn't.

JOHN: Why?

FRANKIE: Kiss me, John, if you want to, but not like that.

JOHN: Why?

FRANKIE: I'd rather you didn't.

[*They stand close, untouching and silent* . . . MR. FREEMAN *comes in.*

MR. FREEMAN: Hullo! Sorry! Thought you were upstairs. Your father's back; the car's out there. But, look here, you stay for a bit if you like. John can walk home with you.

FRANKIE: I think I'd better go with Dad.

[*The gate wails and screeches—*JOHN *hurries to the window.*

MR. FREEMAN: Who's that?

JOHN: Colin come back.

MR. FREEMAN: Who's Colin?

JOHN: The man who was here just now.

MR. FREEMAN: What's he come back for?

JOHN: I don't know.

[MRS. FREEMAN *comes in.*

MR. FREEMAN (*family curiosity*): Where's Gwen?

MRS. FREEMAN: Gone out to the car with Mr. Sewell. Are you going to stay, Frankie?

FRANKIE: I think I'd better go back with Dad. . . . Good night, Mrs. Freeman.

MRS. FREEMAN: Good night, dear. (*A kiss.*)

FRANKIE: Good night, Mr. Freeman—good night, John.

JOHN: Good night, Frankie.

[GWEN *enters.*

GWEN: What a topping car.

FRANKIE: We've only had it a week.

GWEN: Can you drive it?

FRANKIE: Rather.

[JOHN *makes his escape.*

GWEN: I like it heaps better than the old one.

FRANKIE: I should think so. Is Dad waiting?

GWEN: He's gone.

FRANKIE: Gone?

GWEN: I thought you were going to stop.

MR. FREEMAN: You'll have to now.

GWEN: Who was that on the doorstep?

MR. FREEMAN: That feller's come back.

GWEN: It's dark out there; I began talking; I thought it was you at first, Frankie.

MR. FREEMAN: It was that feller.

GWEN: Oh no, it wasn't.

MR. FREEMAN: Eh? Then who was it?

[GWEN *scents danger.*

GWEN: Oh, nobody.

MR. FREEMAN: What d'you mean—nobody?

GWEN: Nobody we know.

MR. FREEMAN: D'you know that feller?

GWEN: Yes.

MR. FREEMAN: It wasn't him?

GWEN: Er . . . no.

MR. FREEMAN: Then why the deuce did he say it was? You thought it was Frankie. Was it a man or a woman?

GWEN: Oh, father, it wasn't anybody we know.

MR. FREEMAN (*under his breath to his wife*): Take 'em into the drawing-room.

MRS. FREEMAN: Let's go into the drawing-room, Frankie—it's so much nicer there.

[FRANKIE *is ushered out.* GWEN *is following, but :*

MR. FREEMAN: Gwen!

[GWEN *stops.*

Shut the door!

[GWEN *does.*

Who let her in?

GWEN: Rosie!

MR. FREEMAN: Send Rosie here.

GWEN: Oh, father!

MR. FREEMAN: Send Rosie to me.

GWEN: Oh, my goodness.

MR. FREEMAN: Will you please not say " Oh, my goodness " to me. . . . Go and tell Rosie I want her.

[GWEN *goes out. . . .* MR. FREEMAN *pulls the scented letter from his pocket, smells it, and with an*

39

exclamation of disgust flings it on the table. . . .
Rosie *comes in.*

Did you show anybody up to Mr. John's attic just now?

[Rosie *is silent.*

Did you?

Rosie: Yes, sir.

Mr. Freeman: Was it a man or a woman?

Rosie (*loyally*): It was a friend of Mr. John's.

Mr. Freeman: Was it a man or a woman?

Rosie (*sticking to it*): I don't know 'oo it was.

Mr. Freeman: She's up there now? . . . is she?
. . . what's the matter with you, girl? . . . is she?

Rosie: I don't know, sir.

Mr. Freeman: Is this thing mended?

Rosie: I don't know, sir.

[Mr. Freeman *gets up and blows in the speaking-tube like an amateur trombonist or an irritated typhoon—and listens . . . evidently no answer . . . another blow . . . and another . . . then another listen . . . still no answer . . . he hangs back the tube and flings from the room . . . slamming the door after him . . . he returns to pick up the offending letter from the table and bear it with him from the room. . . . Rosie remains, sniffing pathetically . . . she creeps from the room.*

Curtain

End of Act I

ACT II

ACT II

UPSTAIRS

The attic that has been in turn JOHN'S nursery, his school-room, and is now his flat. Plain distempered walls; a few pictures—some reproductions of Orpen and Augustus John, and of a Nevinson war picture called " The Doctor "; books; some statuettes; a baby grand piano, littered with manuscript music; two tennis racquets and plenty of comfortable places to sit. The fire-place, which has been converted to a gas-stove, is in the middle of the footlights—that is to say it is imagined—but the chairs are placed so that a group sitting round the imagined gas-fire, sit directly facing the audience, and quite intimately close to the footlights. Two doors; one into his bedroom, the other on to the landing at the head of the staircase.

ROSIE shows in TOBY. TOBY is in the chorus of a musical comedy in a West End theatre. Slight and very pretty, with fair hair and large blue eyes. If you were to talk to her at all confidentially, she would tell you that she thought musical comedy silly, and the other girls in the chorus awfully empty; indeed she has a good deal of sense—but not of her own. Often she could have " got off " with middle-aged business men with money, or with young men with well-brushed hair and incomes; but such were of " no use " to her. Through a curious quality in her she attracts, and is attracted by artists; her life has been mostly in studios and cafés, and from her surroundings, and from the artists that have been in her life, she has acquired her sense and taste.

43

Rosie: This is what we call Mr. John's attic . . . you've got to wait here. I'll tell him. (*She is going; as she reaches the door.*)

Toby: I say!

[Rosie *turns.*]

Isn't there a glass here?

Rosie: A glass?

Toby: Something to see yourself in.

Rosie: Oh! . . . in 'is bedroom.

Toby: In there?

Rosie: Yes.

[Toby *goes into the bedroom.* Rosie *has never seen her before; she looks after her; the tiniest wrinkle of her nose at the door through which* Toby *has disappeared is her criticism. She goes out of the room on to the landing and downstairs . . . somebody is heard on the attic stairs, and* John *comes hurriedly into the room. He stops in the doorway surprised.*]

John: Toby!

[Toby *appears at the door having taken off her hat and coat.*]

I couldn't think where you'd got to.

Toby: I like your bedroom.

John: Do you?

Toby: Who was that I met outside?

John (*with patent anxiety*): Did you meet anybody?

Toby: Yes.

JOHN: Where?

TOBY: On the doorstep; Gwen they called her.

JOHN (*with patent relief*): Oh! She's all right . . . she's my sister.

TOBY: It's nice here. Why haven't you asked me here before?

JOHN: It's nicer in your room—because it's *yours*.

TOBY: I hate you sometimes.

JOHN: Why?

TOBY: When you say things you don't mean . . . you never wanted me to come here . . . you don't want me now. . . . If you think I don't know . . . that's why I've come. If you'd had the courage to say out you didn't want me here, I wouldn't of. . . .

[*He has no answer.*

. . . I wish I hadn't now; coming all up through a great horrid strange house; I nearly went away again.

JOHN: I'm glad you didn't.

TOBY: Why?

JOHN: I'm worried to-night—it's good to be near you. (*He is sincere.*)

TOBY: Is it?

JOHN: Yes.

TOBY: Then I'm glad I came.

JOHN (*getting happier*): Also . . . if you hadn't come, I shouldn't be able to give you something I've got for you.

Toby: A present?

John: Yes. Only I can't give it to you now 'cos you're cross.

Toby: Oh yes, you can.

John: No!

Toby: You'll make me feel a beast for being cross . . . where is it?

John: Shan't tell you.

Toby: What is it?

> [*He shakes his head.*

How large is it? . . . Is it little?

John: No.

Toby: Is it big?

John: Yes.

Toby: How big?

John: Middling.

Toby: Please; I'm not cross any more. (*Whispering very prettily.*) Where is it?

John: Kiss. (*She does.*) Turn round. (*She does.*) On that chair.

> [*She sees a milliner's box, and going to it, undoes it, and extracts an attractive little frock.*

Toby: Oh, you dear! It's the one I saw in Shaftesbury Avenue . . . isn't it sweet? . . . it cost a terrible lot . . . you are *awful* to spend so much money on me. I love it. (*She puts it in a chair to look at it.*) Think I'll look nice in it?

JOHN: Shouldn't be surprised.

[She undoes a button or two in the frock she has on, it slips from her, and there she stands half-naked and unashamed in the scantiest and daintiest of undergarments. She is going to try on her present, but:

JOHN: Come here.

[She does. He puts his arms round her again; she snuggles her head on his shoulder and says softly:

TOBY: Thank you. I'm sorry I was cross.

JOHN: Do you hate me?

TOBY: Sometimes.

JOHN: Do you hate me now?

TOBY: No.

JOHN: Do you love me?

[For answer she looks up and her lips seek his—they kiss as lovers . . . uncannily there is a shrill whistle in the room. TOBY *disentangles herself with wide-open eyes.*

JOHN: Ssssssssh!

[A second whistle . . . and a third, louder . . . then silence; downstairs the enraged MR. FREEMAN *has banged the tube back on its hook.*

TOBY: *What*ever is it?

JOHN: A speaking-tube.

TOBY: A *speaking*-tube? . . . who taught it? . . . what's it say?

JOHN: All clear.

TOBY: Doesn't it want to be answered?

JOHN: No. But it means we're alone here—you and I.

TOBY: Oh!

[*She is near the speaking-tube;* JOHN *has gone to a big chair by the fire.*

JOHN: Put the light out . . . the switch is there by the door . . . there, silly . . . just in front of you . . . that's right.

[*She works the switch; the lights go out—except one softly shaded one.*

TOBY: Oooooooh! Nice.

[*Meanwhile* JOHN *lights the gas-fire!*
[*He holds a match where it should be and there is a terrific bang.*

JOHN: Good lord! These gas fires'll be the death of me.

[*He tries another match—this time with the normal and successful result. He throws a big cushion on the ground beside his chair now in the soft half-light; she comes and makes herself comfortable upon it, leaning against him. They are quiet . . . he caressing her, she gazing into the fire.*

TOBY: It's a funny gas-stove . . . Mabel Claridge has got one like that in her room . . . that man gave her another ring yesterday . . . must of cost *hundreds*. She says there is nothing in it . . . I *don't* think.

[*Her conversation trails off . . . the cushion is comfortable, the heat is pleasant through the flimsy things she has on, and she likes his fingers through her hair.*

It's lovely. . . .

[*She leans luxuriously back towards him . . . he kisses her.*

JOHN: You dear——

TOBY: Thank you.

[*He puts an arm round her, and their heads close, they both for a moment gaze into the fire.*

JOHN: You know . . . I owe you an awful lot.

TOBY: Do you?

JOHN: Yes.

TOBY: How much?

JOHN: Let me think of a few of the things . . . to begin with, everything on the piano's yours.

TOBY (*screwing her head back*): What's on the piano?

JOHN: All my songs.

TOBY: Oh *them*—yes?

JOHN: And you give me *peace* . . . like nobody else in the whole world gives me.

TOBY: Why?

JOHN: Oh, why! . . . 'Cos there's nobody else in the whole world with whom I can be quiet and effortless with all the barriers down.

TOBY: Funny.

JOHN: Just because you can slip out of your frock, like you did, as if I wasn't there and come close into my arms when I ask you, without any fuss.

TOBY (*her face very close to him—her very low voice a lover's*): 'Course there isn't any fuss—'cos I *want* to come close into your arms.

D   49

THE FANATICS

JOHN: That's the wonder of you.

[*Suddenly she shifts her position; kneeling on the cushion she faces him; she shakes her hair with a throw of her head; there is a queer fierce laugh in her eyes—he catches it.*

JOHN: My dear, it's such *fun* loving you.

TOBY: Is it?

JOHN: However much you're loving me I can always see the *fun* of it dancing behind your eyes . . . you've taught me that . . . whatever happens I shall be eternally grateful.

TOBY: What *is* going to happen?

JOHN: I don't know. . . . I don't want anything to happen any more ever. . . . I want to sit here like this for ever and ever Amen.

[*Down in the house there is a little noise—as it were a cloud the size of a man's hand on the horizon—but it grows.*

TOBY: What's that?

JOHN: I don't know.

TOBY: Somebody coming up——

JOHN: It can't be.

[*And the noise grows, as* MR. FREEMAN *falls up the attic stairs . . . there is a knocking at the door.*

Good God!

[TOBY *leaps up;* MR. FREEMAN *getting no answer comes in, and switches on the light. . . . Tableau!*
MR. FREEMAN, JOHN, TOBY.

50

MR. FREEMAN (*after an appalling hiatus of silence, failing to cope with this new situation and throwing the scented letter on to the table*): Yours. . . . Found it among mine.

JOHN (*rattled*): Er . . . thanks. . . . (*Feebly*) This is my father, my father—Miss Clyde.

[MR. FREEMAN *glares speechless.* TOBY *is as if turned to stone.*

MR. FREEMAN: I'll see you about this in the morning. (*At the door he turns and starts to speak.*) Frankie—— (*He gets* TOBY *in his vision again and collapses.*) No, never mind . . . I'll see you in the morning.

[*Even after the door has shut behind him the situation is beyond words;* TOBY *is still motionless, but there is an ugly look in her face.* . . . JOHN *is the first to speak.*

JOHN: I'm awfully sorry.

TOBY: I'm going home.

JOHN: I'm awfully sorry. . . .

TOBY: My things are in there. (*She makes for his room.*)

JOHN (*between her and the door*): Toby!

TOBY: Let me go . . . I feel dirty all over.

JOHN: Let me come with you—please.

TOBY: All right, only let me get out of this bloody house.

[*She disappears into the bedroom . . . he is staring into the fire when there is a timid knock at the door . . . it is repeated.*

JOHN (*hurrying to the door*): . . . Hullo? Who's there?

> [*The door opens before he reaches it and* GWEN *comes in.*

Hullo, Gwen.

GWEN: I say, did I put my foot in it downstairs with father? I'm sorry.

JOHN: Oh, that's all right.

GWEN: I thought you wouldn't mind me coming up—father told me you were alone.

JOHN: *Did* he?

GWEN: Can Frankie come up?

JOHN: *Frankie!*

GWEN: She's staying the night . . . she telephoned home.

JOHN: Where is she?

FRANKIE (*just outside*): Here I am!

GWEN: It's all right . . . he's all alone.

FRANKIE (*her head in at the door*): Can I come in?

> [JOHN *gives a glance at the bedroom door which is shut . . . and* FRANKIE *comes in.*

John . . . can I speak to you?

GWEN (*tactful*): I'll be in my room. . . . I shan't go to bed; I wish you'd give me a call later.

> [*She is gone.*

FRANKIE: I couldn't go home without seeing you.

> [*From the bedroom comes* TOBY'S *voice.*

TOBY'S VOICE: John! . . . *John!*

FRANKIE (*going to the other door and calling*): Gwen!!

GWEN'S VOICE (*half-way down the attic stairs*): Hullo!

FRANKIE: Come back, please.

TOBY'S VOICE: I'm sorry I was cross . . . it wasn't your fault. I've got something to show you . . . wait a sec. . . .

[GWEN *comes back.* . . .

GWEN: What is it?

[*Silence.* . . . *Then:*——TOBY *comes leaping into the room in* JOHN'S *pyjamas and strikes an attitude.*

TOBY: TA—RA!!!!

[*Again she is struck still and dumb by these two strangers; after a moment's silence, with a real big explosive angry "Damn," she goes back into the bedroom.* . . . JOHN *follows her.*

GWEN: I think it would be better if we went downstairs.

FRANKIE: I'm going to stay here . . . have you ever seen her before?

GWEN: No.

FRANKIE: Do you know who she is?

GWEN: No.

FRANKIE: She's common, isn't she?

GWEN: I didn't notice. . . . Frankie, I'm sure we'd better go downstairs.

FRANKIE: I'm not going.

[JOHN *comes in and begins hunting about.*

53

GWEN: What is it?

JOHN: Have you seen a dress about?

FRANKIE: A dress! What sort of a dress?

JOHN: A little blue one.

FRANKIE (*holding it out at arm's length*): This?

JOHN: Yes. Thank you.

> [*He takes it from her and retires again with it. . . .
> GWEN hovers miserably. FRANKIE is rock-like.*

GWEN (*by the door—persuasively*): Come on.

> [*The other shakes her head. . . . JOHN comes
> back, shutting the door after him.*

JOHN: . . . I'd rather you didn't say anything about it till she's gone, please.

> [*No answer. TOBY comes in dressed again.*

TOBY: Show me down to the front door, please. (*She crosses at once to the other door; JOHN following.*)

JOHN (*low to her*): I can't come with you at once.

TOBY: I don't want you to . . . I don't want you to come any more—ever.

JOHN: Toby!

GWEN (*by the open door into the bedroom*): Frankie!

> [*She makes an enticing movement, and this time
> FRANKIE, more tractable, follows her into the bedroom.*

TOBY: I don't want ever to see you again.

JOHN: It's been damnable for you . . . you make me feel a brute.

TOBY: Damned good thing—you are.

JOHN: But who'll look after you?

TOBY: Thanks, I can look after myself. Don't *you* worry . . . show me downstairs in case I meet anybody. . . .

JOHN: You're leaving your new frock.

TOBY: Keep it . . . you can give it to the next one.

[*She goes . . . JOHN hesitates; then calls into his bedroom.*

JOHN: Gwen.

GWEN'S VOICE: Yes?

JOHN: I'll be back in a minute.

[*He follows TOBY. . . . GWEN comes back into the room.*

GWEN: They've gone.

[*FRANKIE comes back; she is blazing.*

FRANKIE: Oh, I *am* angry. It makes you wonder whether there are any decent men in the world. I didn't know John was a *cad.* . . . (*In a burst of rage*) Oh, the beast! the beast! Oh, it makes me furious. . . . While that—girl was waiting up here for him he wanted to kiss me.

GWEN: Did he?

FRANKIE: Yes.

GWEN: But *did* he?

FRANKIE: What?

GWEN: Kiss you.

55

FRANKIE: No, he didn't.

GWEN: Why not?

FRANKIE: I don't know, he didn't.

GWEN: Why didn't he?

FRANKIE: He didn't.

GWEN: You mean you wouldn't let him?

FRANKIE: He came straight up here to her. . . . Oh, it's so humiliating. . . .

GWEN: D'you think it's altogether his fault?

FRANKIE: Oh, I daresay she had plenty to do with it —you can easily see what sort she is.

GWEN (*ominously quiet*): I didn't mean *her*.

FRANKIE (*with fine ironic scorn*): Oh, if it wasn't *her* fault, I suppose you'll say it's *mine* next.

GWEN: Yes.

FRANKIE: Oh, don't be ridiculous.

GWEN: If I was engaged to a man, and he wouldn't let me kiss him, I'd jolly well go and kiss somebody else.

FRANKIE: Gwen!

GWEN: I would. There are times when you must be kissed.

FRANKIE: Gwen!

GWEN: Well, there are—don't you ever feel like that?

FRANKIE: No; besides *her;* she'd kiss anyone.

GWEN: I don't see why you should say that—perhaps they're in love.

56

FRANKIE: Love! What he feels for her isn't love.

GWEN: It's what I'd want my man to feel for me . . . if ever I have a man in love with me again that I want, I . . . (*But* FRANKIE *is crying.*) Oh, Frankie. (*She goes to her.*) Don't cry . . . I didn't mean what I said . . . yes I did . . . but not to say it like that . . . Frankie . . . it isn't a bit simple.

FRANKIE: Yes, it is. Quite simple. He's been a beast; nothing can alter that.

GWEN: I don't know.

FRANKIE: I do.

GWEN: Such heaps of things are uncertain—that seemed certain——

[JOHN *comes back.*

JOHN (*speaking at once*): Will you talk to me, Frankie?

FRANKIE: I suppose so.

JOHN: Leave us alone, Sis, for a bit.

GWEN: Are they up, downstairs?

JOHN: There's a light in the drawing-room.

GWEN: Can I go in there (*indicating his bedroom*)? I should be cross-examined, and I feel all wrong for them downstairs to-night.

[JOHN *opens the bedroom door for her, and she passes into the room; he shuts the door after her . . . there is a little silence between* JOHN *and* FRANKIE.

JOHN (*quietly, almost tonelessly, speaking facts*): I met her during the war when I was on leave . . . we had

57

supper after the theatre, and I went back to her flat—and stayed there . . . and I've been there, sometimes, ever since.

[*She doesn't answer.*]

. . . I'm very sorry it should have happened like this.

FRANKIE: I never dreamed of anything like it. . . . I trusted you . . . I hate being deceived . . . it's been going on all this time and I never knew it . . . all the time you were with me.

JOHN (*quickly*): But I never made love to you . . . it's been absolutely apart from the rest of my life here. She's never been here before.

FRANKIE: Hasn't she?

JOHN: No. . . . They were two quite distinct relationships, mine with you—and with her.

FRANKIE: I should hope so!

JOHN: I've not made love to you, not because I haven't wanted to, but because you didn't want me to. . . .

FRANKIE: I'm glad I didn't. I don't want to share that sort of thing, thank you.

JOHN: You wouldn't have done.

FRANKIE: What do you mean?

JOHN: If you'd wanted to make love, I shouldn't have wanted anybody else.

FRANKIE: That's easy enough to say now.

JOHN: I've been wrong. I've let things drift.

FRANKIE: Why?

JOHN: All this time, I've hoped something would flare up between us, and then it would have been perfect —but it hasn't.

FRANKIE: You say it's my fault too!

JOHN: It's nobody's fault. We're different—that's all.

FRANKIE: Do you want to marry this girl?

JOHN: No.

FRANKIE: I don't understand——

JOHN: Frankie, don't cry.

FRANKIE (*through her tears*): And this morning I was talking to mother about furnishing . . . and the little house . . . it's arranged, nearly . . . what'll everybody say? Oh, it's too bad of you!

JOHN: I'm awfully sorry; I ought to have had it out before; I'm sorry; don't cry. . . .

FRANKIE: Don't talk then.

[*But she cannot stop the tears and escapes from the room. The unhappy* JOHN *remaining, throws himself into the depths of his chair; there is a knock at the door.*

JOHN: Come in.

[*It is the little housemaid.*

ROSIE: Please, Mr. John, there's a lady to see you.

JOHN: Oh, my God! Where?

ROSIE: Downstairs—in the morning-room. She's waiting.

JOHN: I'll come.

ROSIE: . . . Please, Mr. John.

JOHN: Yes?

ROSIE: About that blow-pipe . . . it wasn't my fault . . . 'e blowed; I couldn't stop him.

JOHN: That's all right, Rosie. . . . In the morning-room?

ROSIE: Yes, please, Mr. John.

[JOHN *goes out*—ROSIE *following . . . the silence in the room is broken by* GWEN'S *voice from the bedroom.*

GWEN'S VOICE: You're very quiet! . . . can I come back? Can I . . .? John! . . . Frankie! . . .

[GWEN'S *head comes round the corner of the door . . . and is so surprised at the emptiness that she apologises to it.*

Oh, I beg your pardon! . . . I mean . . . (*She comes into the room with a laugh.*) . . .

[COLIN *comes up from downstairs.*

COLIN: Hullo.

GWEN: Hullo.

COLIN: I was told I'd find you up here.

GWEN: Do you know where John is?

COLIN: I met him on the stairs. Margaret refused to come up till she'd heard from his own lips that we were wanted: I came up.

GWEN: . . . Yes.

COLIN: I've got those tickets.

GWEN: Oh, thank you.

COLIN: For to-morrow night.

GWEN: Thank you.

[*Unexpectedly there is an awkward little silence between them . . . it grows uncomfortably.*

GWEN: . . . Won't you have a cigarette?

COLIN (*gratefully*): Thank you.

[*He takes and lights one; she does the same; the horrid little silence hasn't been killed.*

GWEN: It's a long time since I went to the theatre. It *is* kind of you.

COLIN: I'm looking forward to to-morrow night.

GWEN: So am I.

[*The door opens cautiously and* MARGARET HEAL *appears; a woman of about thirty-five; attractive without being strikingly beautiful or pretty; she is looking her best now, in evening dress and cloak.*

MARGARET: Anybody here?

GWEN: Hullo, Margaret. Come along in. What have you done with John?

MARGARET: He's walking round the square.

COLIN: Sounds mathematical.

MARGARET: Yes, it's impossible.

COLIN: Why?

MARGARET: It's raining; and he's got no coat, and slippers. (*To* COLIN.) You ought to go and fetch him in.

GWEN: It would be kind of you.

COLIN: Certainly I will; if I may come back.

GWEN: Of course.

[COLIN *goes.*

MARGARET: There's been trouble; I'm sure you don't want us.

GWEN: Oh yes I do. I'm glad you came.

MARGARET: It's dreadfully late to call; but Colin was so anxious to come back here.

GWEN: Was he?

MARGARET: Something's happened to him since dinner.

GWEN: Oh?

MARGARET: He's unusually easy enough to manage; to-night he was as obstinate as a pig. He would come; said he wanted to see John particularly. And there was only the most expensive box left for to-morrow night. He would get it. It cost him about twelve guineas. I wonder who he's going to take.

[*She has taken off her cloak.* GWEN *takes it.*

Thank you.

[MARGARET *sits.*

What are you doing with yourself these days?

GWEN: Nothing special.

MARGARET: Have you kept on your nursing at all, since the war?

GWEN: No. And then I only ran errands for the nurses.

MARGARET: Did you like it?

GWEN: Rather. It was something outside home I wasn't cross-examined about. I often envy *you.*

MARGARET: *Me?*

GWEN: John often tells me about you, and your office.

MARGARET: Oh!

GWEN: It's a kind of a literary agency, isn't it?

MARGARET: That's the sort of thing.

GWEN: It must have been awfully adventurous—starting on your own.

MARGARET: I had a good training as a secretary. Then an election came and I had a girl to help me, and I found I could boss her. So I got three girls and bossed them—made them work for me, instead of me working for somebody else. Now I've got ten in the office—and several young men.

GWEN: It must be splendid to have built up something like that for yourself.

MARGARET: It's very interesting. The girls are interesting, too; they bring all their troubles to me.

GWEN: What sort of troubles?

MARGARET: Men—mostly!

GWEN: Are you a good sort of person to bring your troubles to?

MARGARET: I've had some of my own—so perhaps I am.

[FRANKIE *comes in.*

GWEN (*surprised*): Hullo, Frankie! . . . you know Margaret.

FRANKIE: Of course.

MARGARET: Good evening.

FRANKIE: I thought I'd go to bed, and then I thought I wouldn't. I should just lie and think; and I heard you come up.

> [*The other two have nothing to say. She goes on; to* MARGARET:

Do you know what's happened to-night?

MARGARET: Vaguely.

FRANKIE: Did you know this girl?

MARGARET: Vaguely.

FRANKIE: Everybody seems to think it's my fault!

GWEN: Frankie! I didn't say. . . .

FRANKIE: Yes you did. So did John.

> [*Again a silence; again she continues:*

I've been crying; I've got that over, now I've got used to the idea. John says he doesn't love me.

> [*Again they have nothing to say; but she encourages them.*

You can say what you like; I shan't cry again.

GWEN (*gently*): He did: I don't think he does now.

FRANKIE (*unexpectedly defiant*): Well, I'm quite sure I don't love him! I was sobbing away upstairs, but I found it was for the drawing-room curtains I'm not going to buy; not for him. Of course, I'm angry and hurt at being deceived. And I don't see why I shouldn't be! . . . But you can say what you like.

GWEN (*suddenly*): Margaret!

MARGARET: Yes?

GWEN: If I ask you some questions—things that'll help me if I know—will you answer them?

MARGARET: If I can.

GWEN: You're not married?

MARGARET: No.

GWEN: Have you ever let anybody love you? You know what I mean. Words are difficult—I don't want to be frightened by them. . . . Have you?

MARGARET: Yes.

GWEN: Just one man, or more than one?

MARGARET: More than one.

GWEN: Tell me about it, with *all* of them, please!

[*A little smile breaks on* MARGARET'S *lips, and the tiniest laugh. Perhaps the audience laughs louder; so much the better, for* GWEN *answers——*

GWEN: Don't laugh, please. I don't mean it to be anything to laugh at. I ask because I want to know. Not about you, but about love. I'm ashamed to be as old as I am, and not know—You have knowledge, and I haven't. . . . So will you tell me, please?

MARGARET: Ask away.

GWEN: When you didn't know anything at all, how did it first happen?

[*A pause. Then:*

MARGARET (*beginning slowly in recollection*): A man I was doing some work for asked me to join a walking party in the Lakes. We started all together. Half-way through, he and I branched off to walk across a pass

E

and meet the others on the other side. I don't know whether he meant to meet them. I meant to. But we didn't.

GWEN: What sort of a man was he?

MARGARET: An enthusiast about freedom.

GWEN: How old?

MARGARET: About thirty. We walked among mountains and talked a great deal, and when it was getting dark, we reached an inn. And there we had dinner, and there we stopped.

GWEN: Did you love him very much?

MARGARET: No. I was curious.

GWEN: Yes.

MARGARET: It's queer. We hadn't got love, which nowadays seems to me the only justification—yet I've never had any regrets.

FRANKIE: Haven't you?

MARGARET: We were full of air and sky, and ideas for making the world better; probably very silly, but quite genuine. And he was very gentle and understanding.

FRANKIE: What happened when you *did* meet the others?

MARGARET: We didn't. We walked in the other direction for a week. Then we came back to London.

FRANKIE: And then?

MARGARET: Then he fell in love with another girl. I daresay he taught her what he taught me. That seems to be his mission in life!

FRANKIE (*indignant*): That's what always happens—weren't you furious and ashamed?

MARGARET: I was awfully pleased with myself! I was living in a boarding-house in Bloomsbury. I couldn't afford a room of my own, or to go out in the evenings. I used to have to sit in the drawing-room with a lot of old spinster ladies, knitting and playing patience and talking scandal. Before the Lakes, I used to think I should go mad, sometimes; but afterwards, when I looked round at them all, there was a sort of triumphant glee in me. I used to say to myself, " I know more about life than you do. Poor old things! "

GWEN: That must have been topping.

MARGARET: It was rather.

GWEN: . . . Who was the next?

MARGARET: I fell in love; so it's not easy to talk about. I lived with him. For three years. The best time of my life. That's all.

GWEN: D'you mind my asking?

MARGARET: Of course not. Most people like talking about themselves.

GWEN: Why didn't you marry?

MARGARET (*painfully*): We meant to get married . . . when we could afford children. And then I ended it.

FRANKIE: You?

GWEN: How?

MARGARET: At least it was my fault. My man was away; and a boy fell in love with me; it was in the middle of the war when it seemed it would go on for ever. We

67

met at a friend's house; he was in khaki; at a house party. And then he came to have tea with me at my flat.

GWEN: Were you in love with *him?*

MARGARET: I couldn't have married him. But he was very strong, and good-looking . . . and going back to the front. They knew what they were going back to, and they laughed. He was the first man younger than I was who told me that he loved me; and on his last night in England, as if he was my child, I wanted to give him everything he asked for. And he asked for me and—I was glad.

GWEN: I'm glad you were. Did he stop at your flat?

MARGARET: We went to an hotel. We had dinner in the West End. Across the little table—with a shaded light on it—I kept catching him looking at me. . . . One evening when nothing mattered but our happiness. Then he went back to France, and I went home and told my man—and my life smashed.

GWEN: Didn't he understand?

MARGARET: Oh yes, he understood. We went to the Queen's Hall the night I told him, and when we got home talked till five in the morning; it didn't smash all at once—it just made a difference.

GWEN: I don't understand.

MARGARET: Nor do I—altogether. *He* had an affair soon afterwards. You see, he'd given up everything of that sort for me, and I didn't . . . so he didn't . . . it broke up our life together. Freedom's a devastating thing . . . a few hours I shall never forget, and a year of hell afterwards, and I've never really made up my mind whether I'm glad or sorry. . . . (*To* FRANKIE) Do you disapprove of me very much?

FRANKIE: Disapprove? No. But I don't think it's right.

GWEN (*a quick challenge*): What's right?

FRANKIE: When I marry I shall have kept myself for him, whoever he is. And I hope he will, too.

MARGARET: Oh, my dear!

GWEN (*alert*): Why did you say " Oh, my dear " like that?

MARGARET: Another young man fell in love with me. (*She turns to* FRANKIE *with a smile.*) I'm sorry! I know it sounds *dreadful* saying them one after the other, quickly, like this! But there was a year of being lonely—desperately lonely. And it hurt the young man, too; so I let him take me away.

[*A pause.*

GWEN: . . . Well?

MARGARET (*to* FRANKIE): He was one of your ideal young men.

FRANKIE: Yes?

MARGARET: And not only innocent; ignorant. He knew his own needs, vaguely; not mine, at all. I suffered from his ignorance. . . . But he taught me something.

GWEN: What?

MARGARET: Why so many married women go on regarding love-making as horrid.

GWEN: Why?

MARGARET: They're married to men who don't know how to make love. You see, without gentleness and sensitiveness and consideration—and much that comes from knowledge, what ought to be complete harmony can be very disharmonious, what ought to be utterly satisfying to body and soul can be utterly nerve-racking and unsatisfactory. . . . Somebody said that a man who can't make love is like an Orang-Utang playing the fiddle. . . . It wants learning—the fiddle.

FRANKIE: It seems so horrid to make that part of it so important.

MARGARET: I daresay it's not so important if it's right. It's all-important if it's wrong.

GWEN: How?

MARGARET: If you can't make love beautiful for your man, sooner or later, he'll go to someone who can; or he'll want to, which is as bad.

FRANKIE: Are you happy?

MARGARET: I suppose not, really.

FRANKIE: What do you want?

MARGARET: A man of my own, and children.

FRANKIE: Doesn't that prove your way's wrong?

MARGARET: I'm not saying it's right or wrong. Gwen asked me. I've told you.

GWEN: Thank you.

[COLIN and JOHN come in.

Come in and sit down.

MARGARET: If she asks any questions, don't you answer!

70

COLIN: What sort of questions?

MARGARET: Don't ask me.

GWEN: I wish somebody'd tell me what love is.

JOHN (*sotto voce, getting out of his wet coat, disappearing into his bedroom with it*): A damned nuisance.

COLIN: *I'll* tell you.

GWEN (*eagerly*): I should like to know what *you* think.

[*Thus challenged,* COLIN *collects himself; he joins the group round the fire.*

COLIN: As one gets older, and loses one's illusions——

MARGARET: They're off.

COLIN: And realises half one's life has gone, and there's an end to it some day, one is apt to get lonely. A lost atom in an infinity of blackness. In that blackness is despair. Only one thing can dispel it—Love. Real love. None of your free sort, John!

GWEN: What d'you mean?

COLIN: I mean that love between two people that doesn't need anything else, that won't tolerate anything else, that's lasting and tyrannical and jealous, is the only kind that's worth while.

JOHN (*reappearing*): What he really means is, he's getting middle-aged.

COLIN: Real love isn't free.

JOHN: Now listen, Grandpa; you're nearly forty.

COLIN: Shut up.

JOHN: You've been at it twenty years. Have you ever had an experience which might be called free?

71

COLIN: Don't be silly.

JOHN: You've passed the years of adventure, and you want to settle down. So you say: "Ah, I'm wise and sane and right, and all you poor young people are wrong."

FRANKIE (*very much at* JOHN): Do you think you know all about it because you're wrong?

JOHN: We couldn't very well make a worse mess than they have, could we?

FRANKIE: I'm not so sure.

JOHN: Oh, Frankie! If we sat down with a pencil and paper and tried to work out a really unclean, intolerant, silly system, we couldn't work out a worse one than exists to-day. Do you realise that?

FRANKIE: No, I don't.

JOHN: I could make you.

GWEN: Try—go on.

JOHN: Well—to start with . . . the obvious things. (*He talks without difficulty, speaking what he has thought about.*) Hundreds of thousands of girls on the streets; and an incredible amount of sex disease. One in every five infected! A million or so girls more than men doomed to a life without love. Some millions of separated people living without love and not allowed to marry again. Thousands of marriages where only distaste, and hate, remain. Ugliness, and cruelty, and intolerance about the whole subject that makes the sum of unnecessary suffering almost incredible. Does all that sound like a success? After all, we're responsible to the next generation for the sort of world they'll find. Have we any right to say, " Oh, that's all right; we can't do better than that. We needn't bother "? Look at all the girls in the world, Frankie—one lot selling themselves to any man who can pay them; the rest brought up in a sort of prison of asceticism, as candidates for the privilege of becoming a man's married housekeeper.

COLIN: Oh, come, John! Nowadays there are a great many " betwixt and betweeners," as it were!

JOHN: The whole thing's breaking up.

COLIN: Then why bother?

JOHN: The break-up is all so undirected and casual.

MARGARET: Are you so sure it is breaking up?

JOHN: Yes. Quite.

GWEN: Why?

JOHN (*definitely, and as the result of previous thought*): The Church is losing its influence.

COLIN: I shouldn't have thought that mattered tuppence.

JOHN: It's fundamental.

COLIN: How?

JOHN: For hundreds of years the Church has had the most enormous influence by its hold over the lives of men and women in this way. Hasn't it?

COLIN: Yes.

JOHN: Obviously its attitude towards the whole thing is fundamental.

COLIN: Yes.

73

JOHN: It regards sex as sin. It's holy when the Church permits it in matrimony; and then it's got to remain holy, for ever and ever Amen.

GWEN: As if it did.

JOHN: They couldn't stop people loving outside their rules; but they've made them ashamed of it. They've made sex a secret furtive thing. Well, anyhow, we've got *our* chance now.

MARGARET: Why *now*, particularly?

JOHN: The Church built the system, and as a binding force it's no longer effective. Here's your society—in a certain mould; but the power that did the moulding, that held it together, has gone. It's vaguely keeping its shape, at present—but it's crumbling. It must crumble; and it'll have to be remodelled. That was going on, anyhow. Then the war came. Everything shaken to its foundations. Personal beliefs, institutions—everything. The world's fluid. That's why it's all so damnably important now.

FRANKIE: If it's all as bad as you say, surely if people lived as Religion tells them, all these terrible things wouldn't happen?

JOHN: That's exactly what the Church says. " Society must be purified. Men and women must be taught not to sin." But what they mean by purifying society is simply forcing it back under the old rules; what they mean by Sin is any infringement of those rules. What we say is: it's the very narrowness of their rules that has made the mess, it's the reverse side of their mistakenness . . . " they make of their bodies a rampart for the protection

74

of respectable families "—that's what Balzac says of prostitutes. "Sacrifices on the altar of monogamy "— Schopenhauer. Prostitution means disease. You *can't* do away with these things by the old rules. The old rules are the *cause* of them. Practice proves it: the countries with easier divorce laws don't have more promiscuity; less. You *must* tackle the business with new ideas— anyhow, it's happening——

GWEN: What's happening?

JOHN: Compare the world of to-day and the Christian ideal of morality; a man must love one woman and one woman only; a woman must love one man and one man only; *there must be no sex experience of any kind before or after marriage.* That's the ideal. And it's tremendously important to realise it is the ideal; because either you agree with it and you've got to strive ruthlessly towards it, or you don't agree with it, and you've got to find another.

FRANKIE: Are you so certain decent people don't live according to it?

JOHN: Yes.

FRANKIE: I'm not.

JOHN: Take any average collection of people—take any ordinary audience at a theatre! How many men do you suppose have loved only their wives?

COLIN: One or two, with luck.

JOHN: How many women do you suppose have loved only their husbands?

FRANKIE: All of them. There may be just one or two who haven't.

75

MARGARET: You're an optimist.

JOHN: Anyhow, there are more of them every day; it's a matter of mathematics.

GWEN: What *do* you mean?

JOHN: Decent men don't pick up girls off the streets. They love decent women. But if decent men love decent women—where are the decent women? All over the place.

COLIN: If you had the rearranging of the world to-morrow what would you *do?*

MARGARET: I'm going home.

GWEN: Not for a minute. Go on, John. What would you *do?*

COLIN: A minute to recreate the world, John. Hurry up.

JOHN: It comes down to a question of personal responsibility. When outside rules go, inside rules have got to take their places.

GWEN: Yes.

JOHN: I mean, life was probably fairly simple to the early Victorian girl. She was brought up entirely without any sex in her life, waiting for a man to marry her. Anything else was so unthinkable that she didn't think about it. The rules of her conduct were imposed from without. She had no decisions to make. So she didn't worry. It's different now.

GWEN: It is.

JOHN: She's got no respect for the outside rules; she's got to find her inside ones. She *is* worrying. Whether you like it or not, she is. A great deal. Talking, thinking, deciding. Not always as her elders would like. But there are some fine people among 'em; they'll do the devil of a lot to make a better world.

GWEN: I hope that's true.

MARGARET: They're claiming a good deal more out of life.

JOHN: Why shouldn't they?

GWEN: Hear, hear!

COLIN: You're a dangerous influence, young man.

JOHN: To you old men; I hope so; you've been damned dangerous to us!

FRANKIE: If Religion's going to have nothing to do with your new world, what is?

JOHN: You're mixing up religion and the Church. There's got to be a religious spirit; that's essential; I mean the spirit that makes you strive to do the best with your life. I believe some young people to-day want to live according to their beliefs with a sincerity that's religious—anyhow it's causing nearly as much trouble.

COLIN: A lot of conscientious consenters, that's what you are.

GWEN: Now let's be *personal*.

JOHN: Go ahead.

MARGARET: Must we!

FRANKIE: *You* needn't talk.

MARGARET: Needn't! But I did.

77

GWEN: I know I'm sick of living at home; I know I'm sick of living alone. The obvious way out is to get married. But I don't see how I can ever be certain of wanting to live all alone with the same person for the rest of my life.

COLIN: When you're in love, you'll know all right.

JOHN: That's easy to say when you're forty.

COLIN: You're being very unpleasant to me to-night.

JOHN: I agree with Gwen. Nobody can know until they've tried.

GWEN: What d'you mean, " tried "?

COLIN: Oh, my God, where's a drink?

[*He gets up to help himself to one.*

JOHN: Frankie, it's been on the tip of my tongue during these last months to ask you where you wanted to go most in all the world: and then to ask you to come with me there, straight away.

GWEN: What fun! Would you have gone?

FRANKIE: Of course not.

GWEN: I don't see why. A sort of trial affair.

JOHN: No, Gwen. Much more respectable than that. Not a trial " affair." A trial marriage. We should have gone definitely to find out whether we were suited for life.

FRANKIE: That would have been all very nice for *you!*

JOHN: You flatter yourself. It might have been nice for you, too!

78

FRANKIE: Supposing you'd taken me away and left me—where should I be then?

COLIN (*with his drink*): That depends where you went to.

GWEN: Answer, John.

JOHN: If we parted it would mean it wasn't successful. It would be a very good thing for both of us that we weren't tied up for life.

FRANKIE: Anyhow, you'd see a good deal of the world, John!

JOHN: What do you mean?

FRANKIE: You'd always be going away with different people all over the place.

JOHN: This is becoming too personal.

FRANKIE: You began it.

JOHN: Somebody asked me to rearrange the world; and I'm doing it. I certainly wouldn't sweep away all existing marriage laws all at once——

COLIN: When are we coming to what you *would* do?

JOHN: I should go all out for a much larger tolerance; I should allow certain special relationships, *within* the present system, to be open and decent and honourable.

FRANKIE: There *is* something else.

GWEN: What?

FRANKIE: . . . It's difficult to say.

COLIN: Good heavens! Somebody's found something they can't say. It must be awful.

79

GWEN: Go on, Frankie.

FRANKIE: Well—if you go away with somebody—and it's a failure, and you part, for the girl it's not just as you were, is it?

JOHN: No. I see what you mean . . . it seems to me, chastity is a thing nobody has any right to inflict upon anybody else.

GWEN: Hear hear.

JOHN: It may be fine when it's undertaken from real personal belief, but it's not worth tuppence when it's meant a tremendous effort of starvation that achieves nothing but starvation.

MARGARET: You know a lot of girls are quite tranquil and untouched by all this, until it's thrust under their noses.

FRANKIE: That's it. That's where you're so wrong, John. You don't save girls from trouble, you *make* it for them.

GWEN: Quite a lot *aren't* tranquil. It's wicked to keep people from love, when you needn't.

JOHN: Surely you have to deal with every case on its merits. When I have a daughter——

FRANKIE: When you have a daughter, you won't be talking like this.

JOHN: I shall want my daughter to be happily married; *and this is the real answer to you, Frankie.* If you want a happy, lasting marriage, the love-making part of it has got to be successful.

MARGARET: Yes.

JOHN: It's fundamental. Bed-rock. The rock on which most marriages split, and up to now it's been just left to chance . . . a girl must have absolutely no real emotional experience until she's married. Her first real experience may alter her whole being, yet by the time she's allowed that first experience she must have tied herself up for life. Now I don't think that's merely silly. *I think it's definitely wrong.*

COLIN: I agree with you.

JOHN: Grandpa agrees with me. I must be right.

COLIN: Yes, my child, but I think you've got to be extremely careful over this experimenting business of yours.

JOHN: Why?

COLIN: You've got the artistic temperament, God help you. Most people haven't. The majority of ordinary respectable human beings just want quiet, uneventful, peaceful lives.

FRANKIE: Yes.

COLIN: You can just as easily wreck people's happiness by persuading them to go experimenting all over the place, as by denying them the right to do it.

GWEN: Don't just say " Don't, don't, don't." That's negative . . . a denial of things. We can't live by that.

COLIN: My dear—Miss Freeman, I'm not denying the years of adventure, as John calls them. Anyhow, they'll remain for a good many, whatever we say. But when it comes to arranging a new system, keep adventure for adventure's sake for the unfortunate artistic people.

F

They'll hurt themselves. And make a song about it. But if ordinary people get into the habit of fluttering from experience to experience they damned easily lose the stability or the capacity for happiness. And undisturbed love between two people is the highest happiness.

GWEN: But supposing you don't find it, or make a mistake the first time?

COLIN: I'm not denying the right of the ordinary person to experiment, but it ought to be for the definite object of discovering a true lover, and making a lasting marriage.

JOHN: And if you help people to find their real mates, and when they've made a mistake, help them out of it quietly and decently, you'll have many more happy marriages and much less beastliness.

COLIN: Yes, I agree.

MARGARET (*rising*): Well, I'm glad we've settled *that ! !* Now I'm going home. Good night, Gwen.

GWEN: Good night.

MARGARET (*to* FRANKIE): Good night . . . don't think me an abandoned woman——

FRANKIE: I don't.

MARGARET: Good night, John.

JOHN: I'll come down.

COLIN: Got a cigarette, John?

JOHN: There's a new box on the table by the bed.

[COLIN *goes into the bedroom.*

MARGARET (*at the door*): It *is* dark.

GWEN: I'll put on the light; it's just at the bottom of the stairs.

[*They both disappear.*

JOHN (*alone with* FRANKIE): Please . . . will you forgive me?

FRANKIE: I hope you'll find someone and be very happy.

JOHN: I hope you will, too.

[COLIN *comes back into the room.*

FRANKIE: Good night, Mr. Mackenzie.

COLIN: Good night.

JOHN: I'm just going to see Margaret out.

[*He follows* FRANKIE *from the room.* COLIN *alone.* GWEN *returns.*

COLIN: Hullo!

GWEN: Hullo!

COLIN: I'm glad you've come back.

GWEN: Are you?

COLIN: I suppose you wouldn't care to come for a walk with me to-morrow afternoon?

GWEN: Yes.

COLIN: Where can we go in an afternoon?

GWEN: Anywhere.

COLIN: If I came for you in a car about ten, we might get down to the sea and back in time to dress for dinner and the ballet.

GWEN: That would be lovely.

COLIN: Will you be ready at ten?

GWEN: Yes.

COLIN: Ten o'clock then, to-morrow morning.

[JOHN *comes back.*

COLIN: I'll be getting along. Don't come down. Good night, John.

JOHN: Good night.

COLIN (*to* GWEN): Good night.

GWEN: Good night.

[COLIN *goes.*

JOHN: I wish they'd stayed. We might have had a decent talk! I'm going to do some work.

GWEN: I'm going to bed.

[*As she goes, she takes an enormous handful of cigarettes from the new box which* COLIN *had brought in from the bedroom.*

JOHN (*noticing*): Have a cigarette?

GWEN: No, thanks. I don't smoke. Good night, dear.

JOHN: Good night. Bless you.

[GWEN *goes.* JOHN *settled down in a comfortable chair to a book, he gets up to find sheets of manuscript paper, a pipe and tobacco, and throws the lot down beside the chair, and gets into it again . . . his father comes into the room.*

MR. FREEMAN: There you are.

JOHN: Yes?

84

MR. FREEMAN: There's just one thing I want to say to you to-night.

JOHN: Yes?

MR. FREEMAN: Not a *word* of all this business to your sister.

CURTAIN

END OF ACT II

ACT III

ACT III

Downstairs Again

A week later. MR. *and* MRS. FREEMAN *have just finished tea. She is sewing; he is moving about.*

MR. FREEMAN: There's going to be a first-class row in this house this afternoon. A first-class *row.* . . . Is he up there?

MRS. FREEMAN: I think so.

MR. FREEMAN: Having tea?

MRS. FREEMAN: It's Florence's day out. He has his tea down here on Thursdays.

MR. FREEMAN (*at the speaking-tube*): Hullo! . . . John! *Is that you?* Are you up there! . . . What d'you mean "*No!?*" . . . I want a word with you. . . . When you've had your tea. . . . Yes; it's waiting. (*He comes away from the tube.*) I'll teach him to be funny!

MRS. FREEMAN: Is he coming down?

MR. FREEMAN: Yes. (*He paces again*) . . . came like a thunderbolt; this afternoon was absolutely the first I'd heard of it. . . . I've a good mind to pop round and see Frankie, or her father; shouldn't stay; be back here before he's finished his tea; . . . a week ago; never a word to anyone; a week—I didn't tell you all about that evening; that girl up in his room; when I went in there she was . . . well, never mind—and then this morning, he walks into my office, as calm as you like, and informs me, if you please, he does not intend to marry Frankie. . . . And that's not all. Oh no. Not by any means. He's going to leave the business. . . . Leave it . . . throw the whole thing up.

MRS. FREEMAN: What did *you* say?

MR. FREEMAN: I'm not quite sure. But whatever I said, it's nothing to what I'm going to say! I've had about as much as I'm going to put up with! . . . It's such a dam' bad influence on Gwen, too. . . . D'you realise she's only been in to dinner once this week?

MRS. FREEMAN: Twice.

MR. FREEMAN: Once.

MRS. FREEMAN: Wednesday and Sunday.

MR. FREEMAN: Oh yes. Sunday. Well, twice. . . . Where's she been?

MRS. FREEMAN: Out with Mr. . . . Mr. . . . John's friend.

MR. FREEMAN: The playwriting feller.

MRS. FREEMAN: Yes.

MR. FREEMAN: What! Every night?

MRS. FREEMAN: I think so.

MR. FREEMAN: I ask you!

MRS. FREEMAN: He seems a very nice man.

MR. FREEMAN: Does he?! I don't care how nice he is, when it comes to taking my daughter out six times a week!

MRS. FREEMAN: Five times.

MR. FREEMAN: I've had enough. That's what it amounts to. And my foot's coming down—pretty hard.

(*He goes to speaking-tube again.*) Hullo . . . I want to see you; when you've had your tea; . . . you're not going out? very well; when you've had your tea. (*He replaces the tube.*) I think I *will* just look round and see Frankie; and the old man, if he's in; shan't stay; because I'm coming back to talk to John . . . a fine old rumpus; that's what there's going to be; back almost directly.

> [*He goes out. Alone,* MRS. FREEMAN *sews a few stitches; then rises, presses a bell, and returns to her sewing . . .* ROSIE *enters.*

MRS. FREEMAN: Make a fresh pot of tea for Mr. John.

> [ROSIE *fetches the teapot from the tray, and is retiring with it. At the door, she is stopped by* MRS. FREEMAN'S *voice.*

Rosie! . . . Is anything the matter?

ROSIE: No'm.

> [*She goes out. Alone,* MRS. FREEMAN *sews. . . .* GWEN *comes in.*

GWEN: Is he having tea upstairs?

MRS. FREEMAN: No.

GWEN: Oh, it's Thursday.

MRS. FREEMAN: Did you have a nice lunch?

GWEN: Yes.

MRS. FREEMAN: Was it with Mr. . . . Mr. . . . John's friend?

GWEN: He's got a good many friends.

MRS. FREEMAN: Yes; but you know the one I mean— his special one.

GWEN: I lunched with Colin Mackenzie.

MRS. FREEMAN: Oh yes; that's it: Mackenzie. I never can remember. It's such a difficult name. Nothing to get hold of. If it was Mackintosh . . . rain or toffee; *Mackenzie* . . . Mackenzie . . . he seems a very nice man.

GWEN: Not bad.

MRS. FREEMAN (*rising*): I've ordered some fresh tea. I'm going into the drawing-room. (*At the door.*) You'll be in to dinner to-night?

GWEN: Yes.

MRS. FREEMAN: You won't be going out at all?

GWEN: No.

MRS. FREEMAN: I'm glad.

> [*She goes. . . . GWEN crosses to the speaking-tube, and blows into it; she gets no answer; while she is doing this, ROSIE returns with the teapot. As she puts it down, she gives a sudden little sob.*

GWEN (*gently; but without surprise*): Don't cry.

ROSIE: I can't 'elp it.

GWEN: Would you mind if I told Mr. John?

ROSIE: If you wants to.

> [JOHN *comes in*

JOHN: Hullo, Gwen. . . . Have they had their tea, Rosie?

> [ROSIE, *being unable to answer, nods, and then sobs.* JOHN *looks enquiringly from her to* GWEN.

ROSIE: Go on. Tell 'im.

GWEN: Rosie's going to have a baby.

ROSIE (*utterly pitiful*): It's about finished me.

GWEN (*to her brother*): We can help, can't we?

JOHN: Of course.

ROSIE (*with sudden unexpected vigour; turning on him*): It's all very well for *you*!

JOHN (*taken aback*): Rosie!

ROSIE: Standin' there *talkin'*!

JOHN: But, Rosie.

ROSIE: It's all *your* fault, anyhow!

JOHN: *My* fault!

ROSIE: Yes.

JOHN: *Mine?*

ROSIE: Yes, yours.

GWEN: Oh, John!

JOHN: Rosie, what *do* you mean?

ROSIE: I'd never of done it, if it 'adn't been for *you*. I've 'eard yer. *Talkin'!* . . . " What 'arm is there in it?" "Why shouldn't a girl 'ave a good time?" Next time you tell her that, you tell 'er what'll 'appen to 'er.

JOHN: . . . Is he anybody you could marry?

ROSIE: 'E's married.

JOHN: Oh!

ROSIE: I'm frightened. I am, straight. (*She stares at them, in vague terror.*) You're 'elpless; you know what I mean: you go into the next room, and its everywhere; you can't get away from it. (*Her look seems to hypnotise them; they can find no words. She continues:*) It's bad enough when you're married, and 'ave a 'usband to look after yer; and yer mother's pleased. . . . I can't never tell my mother. I can't tell nobody.

GWEN: You've told us.

ROSIE: Oh, it's all right for *you*, miss—*you* don't know. You can't do nothing. I went to a chemist w'ot 'e told me of—a long way off it was, on a tram—and they as good as kicked me out. Then I goes to a doctor; I 'as to go alone. I rings the bell, and the man w'ot opened the door, 'e looked at me—'e seemed to know; and the doctor said 'e couldn't do nothing. It's finished me.

JOHN: Let's go upstairs. We'll be quieter there.

ROSIE: I've got t' go and 'elp cook. That Florence is out.

JOHN: As soon as you can get off will you come upstairs?

ROSIE: Yes. (*She hesitates. Then:*) . . . I'm sorry— what I said. It's kind o' yer; then, you're *kind* all right . . . and if you're a bit orf, you can't 'elp it; I mean, you can't really *know*—can yer? . . . It's an awful thing to 'appen to anyone . . . you gets to 'ate yerself

GWEN: Oh no. (*She adds, rather lightly to help:*) After all, it might happen to any of us.

ROSIE (*fiercely*): Don't you never let it 'appen to *you*, miss. You take care you *'as* 'im, safe, 'e'll marry yer, before you does anything. Me! I lied awake all last night. Throw myself in the river—that's about what I'm fit for now.

GWEN: Rosie!

Rosie: Well, other girls do, don't they? Nobody couldn't blame me then; p'r'aps they'd be sorry. . . . 'Ere, I must get. That old cook'll be after me. She's a one. Work's something; stops yer thinkin'.

John: As soon as you're finished, you'll come back.

Rosie: Yes, sir.

John (*gently but firmly*): Now, look here, Rosie; you've told us and you're not alone any more. And we're going to stand by you and see you safe. See? Whatever happens, we'll see you safe right through and out the other side.

Rosie: It's kind o' yer.

John: 'Tisn't. We're just all in the world together; that's all. . . . You're coming back as soon as you can get away from cook.

Rosie (*with a ghost of a smile, as she goes*): That cook! She's a one!

[*When she is gone, there is a short silence. Then:*

Gwen: It must be awful.

John: Does this frighten you?

Gwen: It's a bit of a red light.

John: How?

Gwen: Well . . . you've got to remember when you talk about all this, it *does* happen to people. It happened to the eldest Gillingham girl. . . . I didn't know much about it; but she had the most terrible time. . . . You can imagine . . . what Rosie said—*helpless* . . . awful. (*She thinks for a while; then her eyes, wandering, light on the tea-things.*) Do you want some tea?

JOHN: Yes . . . thanks.

> [GWEN *pours out his tea and gives it to him; and pours out her own and, sitting, stirs it, reflectively. These two are very fond of one another, and at ease together; there is a quality of gentleness in their bearing to each other.*

GWEN: . . . It doesn't frighten me . . . really . . . not if you stop to think . . . you needn't have a baby, need you?

JOHN: Nearly everybody, in our class, limits their families.

GWEN: If you make up your mind it's not wrong to love without having children, it's awfully *weak* to change your mind just because someone else has one by mistake, isn't it?

JOHN: That's true.

GWEN: But, Jacko . . . you know . . . all the same . . . the people who are against you would pick on Rosie; they'd say, there's a girl with her life ruined, and her baby's life ruined; and if you had your way, there'd be more and more like her. . . .

JOHN: Fools!!

GWEN: Yes, but what's the answer, Jacko?

> [*She speaks, and listens, always, with a simple direct eagerness for understanding, and points of view.*

JOHN: The answer!

GWEN: Yes.

JOHN: . . . Well . . . in the first place: there are plenty of Roses, now, aren't there?

96

GWEN: I suppose so.

JOHN: Thousands. The streets are strewn with their petals; and the winds that strew them, blow out of unhappy homes.

GWEN: Yes.

JOHN: Out of unsuccessful marriages; and lonely separations. They can't boast such a success with their Roses, as things *are*.

GWEN: No.

JOHN: And in the second place, if Rosie 'd been *your* daughter, or mine, she'd have had a different education about it all. . . . Wouldn't she?

GWEN: Yes.

JOHN: What Rosie knows, she knows from cinemas, and giggling talks with other girls and occasional young men. Whatever "teaching" she's had, has been just *Don't*.

GWEN: Yes. Just "Don't. Don't. Don't; it's wicked," all the time.

JOHN: Exactly; about its real possibilities, and its real dangers, she knew nothing; and along comes this man; and over she goes! . . . If she'd belonged to us, she'd have known what she was doing; either she wouldn't have had an affair with this man at all—he's apparently left her in the lurch—or, if it was a thing of real value in their lives, she wouldn't have had a child; unless she wanted it; and was prepared to face up to the whole business.

GWEN: Yes.

G

JOHN: And in the third place, now that it *has* happened, half her trouble is her *fear*; the disgrace of it. If instead of cursing her, and blaming her, and pushing her away, people would help her, it wouldn't be so very terrible.

GWEN: There's her baby. . . .

JOHN: Gwen; an epileptic woman in a slum can have twelve children by a confirmed drunkard. Which is worse? That; or this baby of Rosie's? But as long as it's in " holy matrimony," people can have dozens of children with no earthly chance of looking after them—and your moralists make no objection; but they'll torture young Rosie till she thinks of suicide. . . . The whole question of children—I'm sure it's a matter of *clear thinking*. It's so damned important we should think clearly. . . . Love between two people is a personal relationship.

GWEN: Yes.

JOHN: I can't see that anybody has a right to interfere.

GWEN: No.

JOHN: But as soon as you have a child, it's more than personal; it's a social relationship.

GWEN: Yes.

JOHN: And the Law oughtn't to be concerned with the personal side of it at all; but with the social—with the obligations to the children.

GWEN: Yes. . . . What would you do about children in your trial marriages?

JOHN: There oughtn't to be any; not until they've set out to be permanent.

98

DOWNSTAIRS AGAIN

[*Up to this point the talk has been quiet; they have been helping themselves, and each other, to their teas.*

[*Now,* JOHN *is impelled from within to move. His own convictions, with the sense of a world in opposition, trouble him; his sentences jerk out: all underlined, as it were.*

JOHN: But it's just because as many permanent happy marriages as possible seems the best way it's so damned important for people to make a good choice . . . with full knowledge . . . and so, with a real hope of being lasting and happy; and to help them *out* when they've made a mistake . . . it wouldn't be so difficult if people would be open-minded and sane about it . . . people just point out difficulties and dangers, and think they've smashed our case . . . of course there'd be difficulties and unhappiness; love's not simple . . . but look at it all *now*. That's what they forget. Look at it *now*. . . .

When one thinks of the Prejudices, and Intolerance; of all the *Righteousness* that stands between us and a happier world, it drives one mad. . . . Have you walked through a slum lately?

GWEN: No.

JOHN: I did; yesterday; . . . thousands of babies rolling about in filth; and you only see them outside, where at least there's a square inch of open sky above them.

Think of them inside. Whole families in one room. The mothers and fathers, growing brothers and sisters, and new-born babies; all together; day and night; in every city in the civilised world. . . . Think of it, for a moment . . . *intimately*. . . . Good God! Talk about

99

leading little children astray. A civilisation that tolerates it ought to have a millstone round its neck; . . . as a matter of fact, it has; the thing itself is a millstone; dragging us down; fast.

GWEN: How?

JOHN: How! Why: if anybody has the quality to rise out of it, he gets on at his job, marries above him and doesn't have children. The worst are pouring out children, the best are more or less barren.

GWEN: But, John, if the worst are increasing so much the fastest, things may get worse and worse.

JOHN: Of course.

GWEN: Then why doesn't somebody *do* something!

JOHN: For various reasons.

GWEN: What?

JOHN: Religion doesn't do anything because it thinks Birth Control wicked. Big Business doesn't do anything, because it wants cheap Labour; the Governments don't do anything because they want soldiers for the next war.

GWEN: The next war!

JOHN: The next war.

GWEN: Jacko, do you think there is going to be a next war?

JOHN: Who's going to stop it? We're all arming again as fast as we can go. Submarines and aeroplanes; blockade and starvation; bombs and poison gas from the air that'll exterminate whole cities at a go! (*He is speaking with great emphasis.*) D'you realise one of the leading scientists of the world has said that the millions of London could be blotted out in three hours! You may say that's an exaggeration; it may be; but at the rate science is going it won't be in a few years. "Easy and inexpensive"— that's what a Cabinet Minister said about poison gas; and they're all making it; as fast as they can go; and fleets of aeroplanes to drop it.

GWEN: Do you mean that the children I may have, or you may have, may be just wiped out in another war, more terrible than the last?

JOHN: Why not? When nations are armed to the teeth, the arms go off, sooner or later. It always has been so; there's no reason why it should be any different now; unless there was a change of spirit; and there's no sign of that. Why should there be? The old ideas are still in power; all over the world; the very same men mostly; you see, *they* survive wars!

GWEN: But can't *we* do something? Why should we have children for that?

JOHN: My dear, they laugh at *us*. And at anybody else who suggests they aren't wisdom incarnate . . . unless we ever became effective against them; then they'd find a way of downing us. You've only got to read the newspapers: speeches by generals, and admirals—and bishops; threatenings by politicians; in every country; the old financial interests at work under it all; and the great mass of the people, in every country, struggling all day just to exist, absolutely incapable of independent thought, and ready to believe what any newspaper tells them three days running.

GWEN: John! . . . if it's like that, what's the good of anything! It doesn't seem worth going on, or trying.

JOHN: Oh yes, it's worth it. If the smash comes the few ideals that are left will float upward, and have some influence on what comes next. Something's got to come next! . . . Men *could* free themselves from war.

GWEN: Could they?

JOHN: And from all the other forces that make them suffer so. They're not natural forces; they're forces men have made.

GWEN: Then why don't they?

JOHN: . . . And it isn't for want of courage or nobility.

GWEN: Then why?

JOHN: There's no *will* to do it, and that's because there's no understanding. . . . I often think, now, of being in the trenches.

GWEN: Do you?

JOHN: There was a joy in it; at first, anyhow.

GWEN: *You* say that!

JOHN: Comradeship.

GWEN: The friends you made. . . .

JOHN: No. The strangers on the road, day and night, at the same task; one's rest and play only to give one strength for it; a *purpose* that gave meaning to every moment.

GWEN: Oh, Jacko, something in me leaps to that.

DOWNSTAIRS AGAIN

JOHN: For five years the men under forty worked together, sacrificed everything they had in life, every hope, prospect, comfort; they underwent suffering, physical suffering and moral suffering, absolutely inconceivable to those who stayed at home, so that to give their lives at the end of it was often a relief . . . and they won! By God, Gwen, if the men over forty with the money and the power would get together and work *one-twentieth* as well, and sacrifice *one-hundredth* of their personal comfort, what mightn't they make of the victory—but they won't! They won't, because they see no reason why they should. They've got no *faith* to make them. They've got nothing great to *believe in.* . . . To-day, the wisest of men are cynical, and the cleverest are rich, and none are happy. . . . There's no great purpose outside our own lives to give them harmony and meaning. Ask the ordinary people, in the streets, and tubes, and 'buses . . . what they're living *for;* they don't know. . . . All the old *duties*—our duty to our parents; to our country; to God; they've been prostituted; they demanded our blood; and took it; and gave us nothing in return but a dreadful sense of futility . . . we've got to find something truer to believe in. . . .

GWEN: Can we find something?

JOHN: I believe so.

GWEN: What?

JOHN: . . . Why not, just . . . our duty to our fellows. . . . Suppose we all started in with that as a *Religion;* with half the will we went to war; a common purpose so deeply felt that everybody was ready to spend their lives for it, and make any sacrifices that were called for; I'd be a parson if that was religion, teaching that common purpose—just to clear up the mess a bit; so that the generation that's waiting just outside the doors of existence, should come in and find it a happier place; it 'ud be a dam' sight happier place for those in it *now*, anyhow! and we'd soon do away with any fear of another war; that 'ud be something.

GWEN: John, do you think there's a hope?

JOHN: There's always hope—in the young people.

GWEN: Do you believe that?

JOHN: What other hope is there? There are millions and millions waiting to be born; they haven't got all the prejudices and hatreds that cause the trouble; they get 'em from us; we've got to give 'em something better.

GWEN: And shall we?

JOHN: If we don't, they'll go through all the hell that we've been through, probably a worse hell than anything we've known yet—in this country, anyhow—and then their children, and their children's children, will try again.

GWEN: But *now!* Can't we do anything now?

JOHN: I don't know.

GWEN: We ought to try.

JOHN: That's what I feel. That's why I'm chucking the business.

GWEN: What are you going to do?

JOHN: Follow my urge! That's all I can do.

GWEN: What's that mean?

JOHN: I've got a few hundred pounds in the bank; and I'm selling my piano, and everything else I can. I'm going to write; and think and read; and get into touch with any others I can, who feel as we do.

GWEN: Yes. What are you going to write?

JOHN: I want to try and write something for the ordinary sort of person, who's just lost and discontented. There *are* some.

GWEN: Heaps and heaps.

JOHN: That might be my job; it's not much; when one talks of *doing*, what can one *do*, oneself, seems so inadequate. But it would have been a poor excuse before a tribunal: " I'm not going to join up." " Why? " " I don't see myself winning the war single-handed " . . . plenty only stopped a bullet going into something else. I may only encourage somebody else to do something.

GWEN: You're lucky having something you know you ought to do. I wish I had.

JOHN: You have!

GWEN: What?

JOHN: There's one way all our lot can help: it's probably the best way, too.

GWEN: What is it?

JOHN: To live by what you believe, which is difficult . . . and not by what you don't believe, which is easy.

GWEN: Yes.

JOHN: If you can, you're a fanatic! But I believe you've got to have something of a fanatic in you to do anything worth while these days. The thing is to keep one's fanaticism, and to keep one's humanity.

GWEN: Jacko! It *is* important to live what you believe, isn't it?

JOHN: *I* think so; tremendously; I think, if this generation misses its opportunity, *which it may*, it's because we've lost the old beliefs and haven't taken the trouble to get a new one for ourselves.

GWEN: Yes. Oh, there are such heaps of people " lost and discontented "; I know such heaps of girls like that. They just don't know where they are; they make an awful mess of things sometimes.

JOHN: You do, if you don't know where you are. You know, if we're not careful, there'll be a period of aimless licence, and then reaction. It's a critical time all right. A puritan reaction; and all the old inhibitions and denials and secrecies *clamped down* on our children again.

GWEN: It makes everything seem unimportant except doing one's bit; doesn't it?

JOHN: Yes.

GWEN: It's funny that just when I'm beginning to feel like that, there *is* something in my life that's important.

JOHN: What?

GWEN: You won't laugh!

JOHN: Of course not.

GWEN: I only wish it didn't seem so important . . . you won't laugh?

JOHN: You'll get a clump on the head in a minute, if you keep on asking me not to laugh . . . what is it?

GWEN: I'm in love.

JOHN: Colin?

GWEN: Oh damn! Is it so obvious?

JOHN: 'Tisn't obvious a bit; up to a second ago I hadn't a notion; but you've seen a good deal of him these last two weeks, haven't you?

GWEN: He's taken me out nearly every day; theatres and dinners; I've never had such a time.

JOHN: Does he love you?

GWEN: I don't think so; I don't think he cares a bit more for me than for all the others he takes about. I'm a fool! I dread every time I see him in case I should find out it's no good; but every time he goes away, life's just waiting for the next time I see him!

JOHN: Are you sure?

GWEN: *Sure?* How?

JOHN: That you love him?

GWEN: Yes.

JOHN: Enough to marry him?

GWEN: Yes.

JOHN: By jove, Gwen, I'd like you to.

GWEN (*brokenly*): Oh, Jacko. . . .

    [*A knock at the door.*

JOHN: Come in. . . . Hullo, Colin!

COLIN (*coming in*): Hullo . . . Hullo, Gwen. Good afternoon.

JOHN: Have some tea? It's quite cold.

COLIN: No, thanks.

GWEN: I'll make some in a moment.

COLIN: You've had yours. . . .

GWEN (*rising*): I'll make some more.

COLIN: No. Don't you go. . . . (*To* JOHN.) Can *you* make tea?

JOHN: Yes.

COLIN: I'll have some if *you* make it.

JOHN: I don't make it in this house; I don't know where the things are kept.

COLIN: Well, could you go and buy some cigarettes?

JOHN: I've got some!

COLIN: Could you run out and post a letter?

JOHN (*with a grin*): I haven't got any to post!

COLIN: Then go out into the street, and go up to the first person you meet, and ask them to teach you to take a hint.

JOHN: You want to be left alone!

COLIN: You're very bright this afternoon.

> [JOHN *goes straight out of the room.* . . . *A sudden silence falls.* . . . COLIN *takes out his cigarette-case, and helps himself to one; and puts it back* . . . *and takes it out again.*

I beg your pardon . . . will you?

GWEN: No, thanks.

> [*He puts it back, and lights his cigarette . . . the silence grows again.*

GWEN: I think I will.

> [*He takes out his case; she takes a cigarette, and he lights it for her.*

COLIN: . . . lovely day it's been.

GWEN: Yes.

COLIN (*suddenly*): I say, Gwen!——

> [*A knock at the door.*

Come in.

JOHN: Sorry! It's raining! I'll be upstairs. Give me a blow when I can come down.

COLIN: Seems a bit changeable!!

GWEN: Yes.

COLIN (*throwing away his cigarette, he starts again with the same suddenness of tone*): Gwen! . . . What would you say if I asked you to marry me?

GWEN: . . . are you being serious?

COLIN: Yes.

> [*He comes quickly to her where she is sitting; he speaks crisply.*

I want to kneel down, but I can't. Stand up.

> [*She does. They are standing close . . . they remain so for a moment, and then kiss.*

COLIN: Then it's all right?

GWEN: Yes.

COLIN: Thank God. I wish I'd said this days ago.

GWEN: So do I.

COLIN: Do you?

GWEN: No I don't. I don't want anything to be different. Oh, Colin, you've taken such a load off my mind! . . .

COLIN (*roughly*): Come here!

[*He takes her and kisses her again; they part; he strides away from her.*

Oh my God! I am happy! (*His eyes fall on the tea-tray.*) Have some cold tea?

[*She shakes her head; he pours himself out some.*

My throat's as dry as a bone. (*He drinks.*) Come to dinner to-night?

GWEN: Yes.

COLIN: And to-morrow?

GWEN: Yes.

COLIN: And lunch?

GWEN: You're lunching with someone.

COLIN: I'll put 'em off.

GWEN: You oughtn't to.

COLIN: Yes, I ought.

GWEN: I'm so glad you will.

COLIN: Oh, my dear!—it's difficult to talk sense. Let's try. I don't want to wait. Do you?

GWEN: I don't think I could.

COLIN: When shall we get married?

GWEN: Not yet.

COLIN: But we don't want to wait.

GWEN: No.

COLIN: Then what do you mean?

GWEN: Don't let's get married yet.

COLIN: Oh don't let's have any more of that *rot!* (*And, because his nerves are on edge, he makes it sound more explosive than he meant. Realising, he adds, mitigatingly:*) I mean, it may be all right when you're not serious, but when you are, it's no good.

GWEN: It's not " rot " to me.

COLIN: Well—perhaps not; but *we* needn't be mixed up in it.

GWEN: Leave it to somebody else.

COLIN: Yes! pray God, yes! Look here, I love you. Please understand that. Quite certainly. With everything in me, for always.

GWEN (*very gently, to herself*): Oh, Colin!

COLIN: I've been very lonely; with everything I wanted—unhappy. You've changed all that. I want everything now, for you.

GWEN (*softly*): It's a miracle!

COLIN: It's a fact. But I know what I want; d'you see? . . . that's going to give me the power to get it— for both of us. All this experimenting business. It's no good. I've finished with it!

GWEN: You've *finished* with it!

COLIN: Yes.

[*She gives a little laugh.*

COLIN: Now, look here, Gwen; people who *shilly-shally* round and get someone in their lives, and then look round and wonder whether someone else wouldn't give them a fuller life! I've no use for it. I know a good deal about life.

GWEN: You mean you've had a lot of . . . of lovers?

COLIN: You know that. I don't want to pretend. Not an abnormal amount! Nothing out of the ordinary, but *because* this isn't new to me, I haven't a doubt. This thing's permanent. I *know*.

GWEN: It's all new to me.

COLIN: Can't you trust me?

GWEN: To teach me love. Yes.

COLIN: Gwen, I've seen my children in your eyes.

GWEN (*with a little cry*): Oh, why did you say that? You know I want them, too; but not yet.

COLIN: My dear love; if you want to see life, or the world, a bit first—of course—there's nowhere you can't go; nothing you can't have for the asking; I'm going to give the rest of my life to give you everything you want.

GWEN: I only want you.

COLIN: That's all right then. Now; when are we going to get married? . . .

[*She is silent.*

Has John been putting you up to this?

GWEN: To what?

COLIN: This refusing-to-marry stunt!

GWEN: No.

COLIN: Yes; he has; you've been listening to him.

GWEN: Well, why not?

COLIN: Why not?

GWEN: Yes.

COLIN: Because . . . because I won't stand for it!

GWEN: You won't stand for it?

COLIN: No. Why should I? Your head's full of his stuff.

GWEN: It's full of his stuff because I believe it's true.

COLIN: Oh, damn it all, Gwen; what d'you believe's true?

GWEN: I believe with all my soul to marry you now, straight off, would be a wrong thing to do. (*She is passionately sincere.*) Really! Really! I don't believe it would be *right!* If I did, it would only be to save bother. I want to do what's right. Oh, I can't talk; I can't say what I mean; I feel it; it isn't only myself . . . it's the others.

COLIN: The others?

GWEN: Yes; we're supposed to; it isn't easy to hold out; some girls are; I want to be on their side; I want to keep hold of my part in the future; if I give in right at the beginning, how can I ever take any part, or interest ever again, without being ashamed . . . if that's a "stunt"; if it's all "rot" to you . . . it's no good; you'd better go!

COLIN: And you say you love me!

GWEN: Yes; I love you; make no mistake about that. I don't know what I shall do, if you go. . . . I love you so much, I don't want our first love to be spoiled by feeling I'm doing wrong.

COLIN: You're obstinate.

GWEN: I can't help it. . . . Oh, Colin, please, don't you see . . . if *you're* certain, it'll make no difference in the end.

COLIN: Oh, it'll make a difference all right!

GWEN: What difference?

COLIN: It's going to be very unpleasant for me.

GWEN: If I'm not more important than unpleasantness——

COLIN: Suppose I'm obstinate too; and just as conscientious; and I don't want it to be spoiled, and I think we *ought* to get married.

GWEN: You don't. You want to avoid unpleasantness.

COLIN: Thanks.

GWEN: It's true.

COLIN: Suppose it's a question of doing things my way, or saying good-bye?

GWEN: Oh no!

COLIN: Yes.

GWEN: Colin! . . . if I gave in, I shouldn't be any *good* to you; something in me would die.

COLIN: I'll risk that.

GWEN: I can't give in.

COLIN: My way, or saying good-bye.

DOWNSTAIRS AGAIN

GWEN: Oh, Colin.

COLIN: . . . Well?

GWEN: Colin!——

[MR. FREEMAN *enters. He has hurried and is in a temper anyhow, which is not improved by finding " that feller " alone with his daughter.*

MR. FREEMAN: Oh! . . . Where's John?

GWEN: He went out.

MR. FREEMAN: Where to?

GWEN: I don't know.

MR. FREEMAN: He's got no business to go out. I want to speak to him. I told him I wanted to speak to him.

[*A whistle from the speaking-tube.*
That's probably him.

[GWEN *has gone to answer. She takes the receiver and speaks.*

GWEN: Hullo!

MR. FREEMAN (*taking it from her*): Here, give it to me. (*He listens.*) . . . Has he " *popped* " what ? No. It's me speaking. *Me.* I don't know what you're talking about. Come down. At once. (*He replaces the instrument.*) . . . What the devil did he mean? . . . Going off his chump! That's what's the matter with him. Off their chumps! That's what's the matter with the whole family.

[*A silence.* COLIN *and* GWEN *are hung in mid-air, as it were; while* MR. FREEMAN *becomes more and more manifestly oppressed with their presence.*

115

COLIN: . . . Well, I must be getting along.

MR. FREEMAN (*jumping at this*): I'm sorry I can't ask you to stay. I've got some particular business to discuss with my son.

COLIN: Oh, of course. (*He hesitates awkwardly a moment, and then says, low, to* GWEN:) Will you come and have dinner to-night?

GWEN: Yes.

MR. FREEMAN (*catching this*): What's that?

COLIN: I was asking your daughter if she'd dine with me to-night.

MR. FREEMAN: I'm afraid I can't allow it.

GWEN: Father!

MR. FREEMAN: *That's enough!* . . . You've been out with Mr. Mackenzie six times this week. I'm sure Mr. Mackenzie's man-of-the-world enough to realise that's unusual.

GWEN: I'm over twenty-one.

MR. FREEMAN: I can't help that. You're in my house; under my charge.

[JOHN *comes in.*

Come in. I've just had to put my foot down. I've forbidden your sister to go out with Mr. Mackenzie.

JOHN: Forbidden!

MR. FREEMAN: Yes. *Forbidden!* If I don't take a strong line, goodness knows where we shall get to. You young people think you can play highty-tighty just as you please. . . . As I say, I've no wish to be offensive to Mr. Mackenzie. It's very good of him to spend so much time on her. . . . Every now and again. Yes. Of course. But six times a week! The thing becomes ridiculous. (*To* COLIN.) I hope you understand my position.

COLIN: I think perhaps you don't quit understand *my* position. I have asked your daughter to marry me.

MR. FREEMAN: This is the first I've heard of it.

COLIN: I only asked her a few minutes ago.

MR. FREEMAN: Well, of course, this does rather alter the aspect of things. . . . I don't know what to say; 'pon my word, you've rather taken the wind out of my sails . . . of course, it's all got to be considered. I shall want to talk to you . . . then, if I approve, and her mother . . . the whole thing wants talking over.

GWEN (*she is very pale, and her teeth are set*): You needn't talk it over, thank you. I've made up my mind.

MR. FREEMAN: Oh, you have.

GWEN: Yes. I've told him I won't marry him yet. But I've told him I'll go away with him; and we can get married later; when I know what I'm doing; if we want to.

MR. FREEMAN (*blankly*): You told him you'd go away with him!

GWEN: Yes.

MR. FREEMAN: I don't understand! What d'you mean?

GWEN: What I said: I told him I'd go away with him. I'll marry him afterwards when I'm sure.

JOHN (*almost to himself*): Gwen! That's good!

117

MR. FREEMAN (*turning fiercely on him*): GOOD!!! What the devil do you mean—*good?!!!* Really, I don't know whether I'm on my head or my heels! (*To* COLIN.) What have *you* got to do with this?

COLIN (*taken aback*): Me?

MR. FREEMAN: Is this the result of six dinners with you?

COLIN (*trying to be dignified*): Certainly not.

MR. FREEMAN: I suppose I can believe my ears. You heard what she said . . . she's already made this outrageous suggestion to you.

COLIN: Yes.

MR. FREEMAN: After any encouragement from you?

COLIN: No.

MR. FREEMAN: Do I understand then that you propose to behave like a gentleman?

COLIN: I'm not quite certain how a gentleman would behave under the circumstances.

MR. FREEMAN: I'm sorry to hear that.

COLIN: Well, how would *you* behave?

MR. FREEMAN: Me?

COLIN: Yes. Supposing when you were single, the girl you loved, out of a sort of access of social duty, had proposed a sort of trial trip before you were——

MR. FREEMAN: Social fiddle-sticks! When I was a young man the thing was unthinkable.

GWEN ⎱ : But Father!——

JOHN ⎰ : When you were young, but——

MR. FREEMAN (*turning on his children and shouting*):
I *will* not argue.

COLIN: I don't want to argue either; but I think you
might answer my question. What would you do in my
place?

MR. FREEMAN: Do! Why, good God, sir, I should
tell her to go to the devil.

COLIN: I'm rather thinking of telling her to do that.

MR. FREEMAN: I'm glad to hear it.

COLIN: Only if she does, I suppose I shall go with
her.

[*A very tiny suspicion of a laugh from* JOHN *is
immediately quashed.*

MR. FREEMAN: *Stop that noise!* Is your sister's *shame*
a laughing matter to you?

JOHN (*dangerously*): *Shame?!*

MR. FREEMAN: Yes; that's what I said—*shame*. It's
time there was a little plain-speaking in this house!! I
don't know what's come over you; both of you. You
think you can treat us just as you like; push us on one side;
me, and your mother, and the family; the traditions;
trample on everything we hold sacred. You can't.

[*The two stand silent, while he looses his wrath
against them. To* JOHN:

You think you can break faith just as you will: you
can't; you throw over the girl you've been engaged to
since you were children; and the same with the business;
and never a word 'till this afternoon . . . and now
this . . . this cruel, insane, folly of Gwen's. A cruel,

119

thoughtless, insane *wickedness* that I never thought I should find in a child of mine. Have you no thought for others—either of you? No consideration? (*To* John.) You're lazy; that's what's the matter with you. No aim in life. No desire to get on. Dog lazy. And you. (*He turns on his daughter.*) You're worse. Are you mad? or are you wanton? You seem to have no thought but for your own pleasure——

John (*going off suddenly, like a bomb*): Be QUIET!!!!

Mr. Freeman: What the devil?

John: I shall lose my temper in a moment.

Mr. Freeman: Lose your temper?

John: Yes. I have lost it. I've lost it now!! How *dare* you talk like that? *How dare you?!?!*

Mr. Freeman (*shouting*): John!

John (*refusing to be stopped*): It's no good. It's got to come out now. *You,* who sat at home here in comfort all those five years of hell.

Mr. Freeman (*bewildered*): Sat at home!

John: You don't know what I'm talking about! You've forgotten. I'll tell you. (*He is possessed by an overwhelming rage.*) Your generation has done ours in! Smashed it! Millions! If we were to stand at that window and they marched past us, they'd march all day, and all night, and all day again—for days and nights. Dead men. Dead. For what? They died to end war; to make a better world; and before their corpses have rotted into earth, new wars are preparing and the world's a dam' sight worse—and you? Is there one word of apology in you?

One word of humility? No. The same old pride; and blindness; and intolerance. Because I don't want to live as you've lived, I'm lazy; because Gwen wants to live, not exactly as her mother and grandmother lived, she's mad or wanton! Good God in Heaven! if there's one way that's been proved wrong it's your way! If we live exactly as you lived, it'll all happen over again! . . .

[He comes to a sudden stop. The silence in the room is complete. He seems to have burnt himself out; and MR. FREEMAN *to be knocked mentally head-over-heels, and to be only partially conscious.* JOHN *breaks the silence in a low voice:*

Sorry. I lost my temper. I've got it again now. . . . I was rude. I'm sorry. . . . We only ask that you should go your way: and leave us to find ours. I beg your pardon. There's no reason why we shouldn't be friends.

MR. FREEMAN: Friends!

JOHN: Yes.

MR. FREEMAN (*to* GWEN): Do you suppose your mother will ever lift up her head again?

GWEN: We could be far better friends when she knows.

MR. FREEMAN: Don't be a fool.

GWEN: We lived in the same house; but we're strangers.

MR. FREEMAN: Who's fault's that?

GWEN: What I believe is part of me, I can't help that. I couldn't be anything but a stranger with anyone from whom I had to hide it. We could be closer now. If *she* will. I'll do my best.

MR. FREEMAN: Rubbish. (*He makes for the door.*) All I can say now is: I shall oppose you with every means in my power. If you persist, not another penny do you get from me—either of you. (*To* COLIN.) And as for you, sir, you're a damned scoundrel!

[*He goes.*

GWEN (*at once, to* COLIN): Oh, I'm so sorry.

COLIN (*taking her roughly by the shoulders*): Look here; you're going to love me; and I'm going to love you, and there's going to be no one else. Do you understand?

GWEN: Yes.

COLIN: Good. Now I'm going to clear out; right out of it, for a bit.

GWEN: What do you mean?

COLIN: Where do you want to go to most in all the world?

GWEN: I only want to be where you are.

COLIN: I'm going to Rome. As soon as I can get a passport. I think you can get a passport quicker than you can get a licence. Shall I get two—passports?

GWEN: Colin!

COLIN: That's all right. John, I'm going to marry your sister.

JOHN: When?

COLIN: As soon as I can get her away from you.

GWEN: No.

COLIN: Well, when we come back to England.

GWEN: Perhaps.

COLIN: Say yes.

[*She shakes her head.*

You little devil. I'm only afraid of one thing.

GWEN: What?

COLIN: You'll make me serious. Then we shall all starve.

GWEN: I shouldn't care.

COLIN: I should.

JOHN: Well. I've had my telegram.

COLIN: What telegram?

JOHN: My man's bought my piano and every other damned thing in the whole attic. So we're in the soup, now, Gwen, both of us!

GWEN: Yes.

JOHN: Good luck to you. (*He stretches out his hand.*)

GWEN (*taking it*): Thanks. And good luck to you.

JOHN: By God, life's *good*, isn't it?

COLIN: There's someone knocking at the door.

JOHN: See who it is.

[COLIN *goes and opens the door.*

COLIN: It's Rosie.

GWEN: Rosie! . . . I'd forgotten! . . . (*With sudden misgiving.*) John, this isn't going to stop us.

123

JOHN (*very strongly*): No. Nothing's going to stop us now.

GWEN: But we must help her.

JOHN: *Of course we must help her*; that's part of our job. . . . Rosie! . . .

[*As he goes to the door the* CURTAIN FALLS.

END OF THE PLAY

Printed in Great Britain at
The Mayflower Press, Plymouth. William Brendon & Son, Ltd.

OTHER PLAYS BY THE SAME AUTHOR

YOUTH
PADDLY POOLS
THE LITTLE WHITE THOUGHT
MAURICE'S OWN IDEA
D. CO. AND BLACK 'ELL
YOUNG HEAVEN AND THREE OTHER
 PLAYS

CONTEMPORARY BRITISH DRAMATISTS

(*Continued from page 2*)

PLAYS OF INNOCENCE. By GWEN JOHN

"*Miss John . . . has Hardy's gift of expressing universal realities through the lips of simple folk.*"—"*Sheffield Daily Telegraph.*"

THE STOLEN HORSE. By CHARLES FORREST

"*A work of quality.*"—*A.N.M. in the "Manchester Guardian."*
"*Shows unusual dramatic talent.*"—"*Daily Telegraph.*"

SONS AND FATHERS. By ALLAN MONKHOUSE

"*A great theme, nobly handled.*"—"*Manchester Guardian.*"

THE MAN WITH A LOAD OF MISCHIEF. By ASHLEY DUKES
(*5th Impression—10th Thousand.*)
"*A very charming and elegant play.*"—"*Morning Post.*"

THE FANATICS. By MILES MALLESON

"*Mr. Malleson has a complete knack of making his folk convincing.*"—"*Spectator.*"

THE CONQUERING HERO. By ALLAN MONKHOUSE. (*3rd Impression.*)
"*I am often asked what I call a great play. This is one.*"—*James Agate.*

THE SCENE THAT WAS TO WRITE ITSELF. By G. D. GRIBBLE

THE THREE BARROWS. By CHARLES McEVOY

"*Strong dramatic scenes, would act well.*"—*E. A. Baughan.*

FIRST BLOOD. By ALLAN MONKHOUSE

"*Deals with a savagely embittered industrial dispute, at once more natural and more subtle than Galsworthy's 'Strife.'*"—*Ivor Brown in the "Manchester Guardian."*

THE DANCE OF LIFE. By HERMON OULD

"*Delightful.*"—"*English Review.*"

THE FIFTH OF NOVEMBER. By HOWARD PEACEY

"*There is colour and eloquence in it.*"—"*Times Literary Supplement.*"

MIDSUMMER MADNESS. By CLIFFORD BAX

"*Mr. Bax has done what the commedia dell' arte did—told a cynical modern story through old figures.*"—"*Times Literary Supplement.*"

THE MASQUE OF VENICE. By G. D. Gribble
" Mr. Gribble is master of his job and possessed of more wit and more reading than most living dramatists."—" Times Literary Supplement."

ATONEMENT. By Edward Thompson
" Mr. Thompson is among the playwrights born."—" Times."

NOCTURNE IN PALERMO. By Clifford Bax
"A delightful miniature."—" Daily Telegraph."

THE RIGORDANS. By Edward Percy
"A play to read."—" Manchester Guardian."

KRISHNA KUMARI. By Edward Thompson
"A play about India and a very fine one."—Robert Graves in the " Nation."

MAGIC HOURS. By Howard Peacey
" Mr. Peacey has the stuff within him of which dramatists are made."— " Observer."

HIS MAJESTY'S PLEASURE. By Conal O'Riordan
"An example of how the romantic play should be written."—" Observer."

THE TRANSLATION OF NATHANIEL BENDERSNAP. By G. D. Gribble
" Frankly written for a select and sophisticated audience."—" Curtain."

PLAYS BY H. M. HARWOOD

THE GRAIN OF MUSTARD SEED.

SUPPLANTERS.

PLEASE HELP EMILY.

THREE ONE-ACT PLAYS.

A SOCIAL CONVENIENCE.

THE PELICAN.
" Captain Harwood can handle a dramatic situation or a passage of wit with the skill of a master."—" Daily Telegraph."

In preparation
THE PIPER LAUGHS. By Hermon Ould

CONTEMPORARY AMERICAN DRAMATISTS

THE VERGE. *By* Susan Glaspell. (*2nd Impression.*)
"*Fresh, curious, and dramatically alive.*"—"*Manchester Guardian.*"

INHERITORS. *By* Susan Glaspell. (*2nd Impression.*)
"*I am inclined to think it ranks with 'The Master Builder.'*"—*James Agate in the "Sunday Times."*

BERNICE. *By* Susan Glaspell
"*Remorselessly, every word striking home, this quiet tragedy works to an end.*"
—"*Weekly Westminster.*"

NOTE.—*The three plays by Susan Glaspell are available in a collected edition.*

MOSES. *A Play, a Protest, and a Proposal. By* Lawrence Langner
"*Entertaining and effective.*"—"*Manchester Guardian.*"

THE SPRING. *By* George Cram Cook
"*A richly imaginative drama.*"—"*Weekly Westminster.*"

TRIFLES *and other plays. By* Susan Glaspell
"*'Trifles' is one of the most poignant, most simple human one-act tragedies we have ever read.*"—"*Observer.*"
"*One remembers few plays in which apparently casual talk opens bigger vistas of human nature.*"—"*Manchester Guardian.*"

THE COMIC ARTIST. *By* Susan Glaspell & Norman Matson

OTHER PLAYS PUBLISHED BY ERNEST BENN LTD

THE DYBBUK. *By* S. Ansky

ANGELA. *By* Lady Bell

DR. KNOCK. *By* Jules Romains. *Translated by Harley Granville Barker.*
"*A sparkling and amusing play.... Great fun.*"—"*Manchester Guardian.*"
"*If some manager does not produce this witty comedy in London our theatre and its public will be losing a very delightful thing.*"—"*Daily Telegraph.*"

BEGGAR ON HORSEBACK. *By* George S. Kaufman & Marc Connelly
"*A very distinguished piece of stage work, interesting from beginning to end, containing beauty, wit, satire and humour.*"—"*Daily Telegraph.*"

THE COLONNADE. *By* Stark Young
"*Mr. Stark Young makes his effects with a beautiful simplicity.... 'The Colonnade' is a remarkable play.*"—*Allan Monkhouse in the "Manchester Guardian."*

THE MACHINE WRECKERS. *By* Ernst Toller, *translated by Ashley Dukes.* (*2nd (cheap) Impression.*)
"*It has power and passion and judgment and pity.*"—*St. John Ervine in the "Observer."*

SHAKESPEARE. *By* H. F. Rubinstein & Clifford Bax
"*The Shakespeare is by far the most lifelike, the most plausible—far excelling either Mr. Shaw's or Mr. Frank Harris's.*"—"*Weekly Westminster.*"

THE FIREBRAND. *By* Edwin Justus Mayer